BESTSELLER BLUEPRINT

How to Write, Publish and
Market a Book That Sells

MICHAEL FRANCIS

Copyright © 2025 Michael Francis

All rights reserved

No part of this book may be used or reproduced, distributed, or transmitted in any form or by any means, including photocopying, recording, or other electronic or mechanical methods, without the proper written permission of the publisher, except in the case of brief quotations apart, embodied in critical reviews and other specific non-commercial uses permitted by copyright law. Use of this publication is permitted solely for personal use and must include full attribution of the material's source.

DISCLAIMER

In this book, I have listed the names and contact details of various products and suppliers I have and continue working with.

The reason I have listed their details is because I highly recommend them.

In some cases, these contact details are affiliate links, and if you purchase or subscribe to their product or service, I may receive a modest commission.

Please rest assured if you invest in any product or service that I recommend, you will not be paying any more than you otherwise would.

Contents

Chapter One Introduction 7

Chapter Two A Word of Warning 15

Chapter Three What We Will Explore in this Book 20

Chapter Four How Traditional Publishing Works 24

Chapter Five The Retail Book Market 38

Chapter Six The Four Pillars of Successful Book Publishing 41

Chapter Seven Your Book Idea 70

Chapter Eight How to Write a Novel 76

Chapter Nine How to Write a Memoir 94

Chapter Ten How to Write a Children's Book 115

Chapter Eleven Title and Subtitle 130

Chapter Twelve Editing your Book 138

Chapter Thirteen Traditional or Self-Publishing? 145

CHAPTER FOURTEEN Formatting 151

CHAPTER FIFTEEN Keywords and Categories 160

CHAPTER SIXTEEN Keyword Strategy 170

CHAPTER SEVENTEEN Uploading Your Book to Amazon 181

CHAPTER EIGHTEEN Other Elements 191

CHAPTER NINETEEN Distribution and Royalties 198

CHAPTER TWENTY Book Launch 207

CHAPTER TWENTY-ONE Amazon Advertising 219

CHAPTER TWENTY-TWO Other Opportunities 228

CHAPTER TWENTY-THREE Summary 2422

Chapter One

Introduction

IT ONLY TOOK me thirty years to be an overnight success.

When I wrote my first book, I sent the manuscript to dozens of publishers and literary agents.

This was back when agents and publishers actually bothered to respond to unsolicited submissions with written replies printed on letterhead stationery.

I would keep all my rejection letters in a manila folder, with the words - 'People Who Will Regret It When I'm Famous' written on the cover.

Mind you, that stopped being funny once the file got more than an inch thick.

Most of those replies were a standard template that read;

> Dear Author
>
> While we read your manuscript with interest, we don't believe it is a suitable title for our current list.
>
> We wish you all the best and every success with your writing.

One day (after eighteen months), I received a letter from Random House that was written and signed by a human being. This person even had a name and a job title. She was a Commissioning Editor.

It read;

> Dear Michael
>
> I am not going to make an offer to publish your book, but you should know that this decision was made with some regret, as I think you have a tremendous commercial writing style.

> What let you down in this instance was insufficient plotting to support your well-drawn characters.

It was always disappointing to receive a rejection letter, but this one left me feeling shattered.

I had written my first novel and was desperately close to achieving my dream of becoming an author with one of the biggest publishing houses in the world, but I fell at the last hurdle.

I didn't know whether to feel encouraged or depressed.

For the most part, I chose the latter.

This was over twenty-five years ago, and self-publishing (as we know it today) was in its infancy at best.

In fact, I'm not sure that eBooks and Kindles were even a thing back then, at least not yet, anyway.

So I just kept working in a real job, satisfying my urge to write at every opportunity, while the Amazon phenomenon and the concept of eBooks, print-on-demand, and audiobooks developed without me.

Eventually, I published that first book as an eBook, a paperback, and an audiobook without any real plan or idea of how to market and promote it.

At the time, I figured, "Well, I'll just put it out there, and the world will beat a path to my door."

That didn't happen.

So, I wrote another book.

That didn't fire a shot, either.

It wasn't until I had published my third title, having read several books, countless blog posts, attended any number of webinars, and enrolled in several online training courses, that I started to get some idea of just what I should be doing and what it was I needed to do.

I am not suggesting for one moment that you need to write three or four books before you can expect to achieve any sort of success.

What you do need to know is how to do it properly, and how to give yourself the best possible chance of writing and publishing a bestselling book.

Mine has been a very long and steep learning curve, and I'm certainly still on it, but the difference these days is that I have a very clear notion of what I am doing.

This book is the culmination of my thirty years of experience, research, study, trial, error, and expense.

Bestseller Blueprint will help you to write a great book, and make it more visible and discoverable on Amazon, to say nothing of other online retailers. It will also present you with a distribution strategy that will ensure your book is available from bookstores and libraries worldwide.

This book will help you to write, publish, and market your book - successfully, enjoyably, cost-effectively, and profitably.

Now, before we begin, I want to present you with an overall philosophy that you should keep at the forefront of your mind as you read this book and throughout your entire writing and publishing journey.

The Bestseller Blueprint Philosophy

Struggling Writers Treat Publishing as a Hobby.

Successful Writers Treat Publishing as a Business.

We will cover traditional/commercial publishing and talk about how to submit your manuscript to publishers and literary agents, together with what you can expect with regard to time frames, responses, and potential income.

We will also focus on the opportunities and processes involved in publishing your own work.

Self-publishing a book is perfectly viable nowadays, and, in my opinion, it is a better option than submitting your work to a traditional publisher.

That may surprise some people, but as you progress through this book, I am confident you will reach the same conclusion.

First, let's discredit a couple of common myths about writing and publishing.

1. There is No Money in Being an Author.   RUBBISH

2. Self-Publishing isn't 'Real' Publishing.   ABSOLUTE RUBBISH

Throughout this book, I will present occasional examples and circumstances that relate to one or all of my books. The intent of including these examples is to present actual examples of what worked for me, just as importantly as those strategies and tactics that didn't work.

Also, if I recommend any product, service, or supplier to you, I am doing so because I use those products or work with those people myself, and I can highly recommend them.

Chapter Two
A Word of Warning

SEVERAL PRODUCTS, SERVICES, and online suppliers offer aspiring authors various marketing strategies, promotional advice, and training. Some of them look very impressive, boasting all sorts of eye-watering success; many are very expensive, and the vast majority of them you want to avoid.

An entire industry has sprung up in recent years, offering support, training, and help to aspiring authors. You only need to Google the phrase Book Marketing to see that.

It is very easy to get sucked into watching any number of 'so-called free' webinars that promise all sorts of tremendous, proven publishing and marketing strategies - everything from utilizing social media to generate pre-orders before you launch your book, to building an email list. These webinars are invariably sixty-minute infomercials from people who devote the last fifteen minutes to presenting their 'fabulous' new training course and their easy three-month payment plan. To say nothing of the special discount that applies if you sign up and pay that same day. Be careful. It's very easy to get drawn in.

And above all, never, ever deal with a so-called publisher that asks you to contribute anything at all toward the cost of producing and publishing your book.

- Companies that ask you to contribute to the cost of printing and distributing your book are vanity publishers, who often masquerade as a division of a traditional publisher and who like to say they have developed a 'hybrid' or 'holistic' publishing model.

- These people market themselves to authors who get no response from traditional publishers and who desperately want to see their books published. They target authors who don't know how to do it themselves or think it's all too hard, and you will rue the day you ever dealt with them.

- And the same goes for people who offer to help you to publish your work. These people will charge you a lot of money to do something you can do just as efficiently and more cost-effectively yourself.

- Legitimate publishers will expect you to contribute time, effort, and money to promote your books yourself, by maintaining an active social media presence, for example. Still, they will never ask you to pay them money.

- If any publisher presents you with an 'offer' that obliges you to pay them any money at all to edit, format, publish, produce, and promote your book, then walk away.

- Last year, a so-called hybrid publisher (based in Australia) called Shawline Publishing collapsed after hundreds of authors had paid them in the region of $8,000 each to publish their books.

- The twisted, cruel irony is those authors had assigned Shawline Publishing the rights to their work, and those rights now rest with the liquidators who wound up the company.

- Not only did those authors lose thousands of dollars, they were at risk of breaking a contractual obligation if they chose to publish those same books themselves or submit them to another publisher.

If you ever have doubts about the legitimacy of any publisher, consultant, software, or training course, here are three valuable resources you can call upon.

- Alliance of Independent Authors:

- Self-Publishing Services Rated:

- Writers Beware:

Chapter Three
What We Will Explore in this Book

- How to write an engaging, interesting, and entertaining book that has commercial appeal.

- If it is a novel, a memoir, or other non-fiction book - at least 50,000 words.

- Obviously, not that long if it's a children's book or poetry.

- Submitting to publishers and literary agents. What can you expect, and how does traditional publishing work?

- The Four Pillars of Successful Book Publishing.

- Editing.

- Proofreading.
- Formatting.
- Book Title and Subtitle.
- ISBNs and Barcodes.
- Cover Design and Formatting.
- Self-Publishing and Distribution - Amazon, Ingram Spark, Draft2Digital & Findaway Voices.
- Print-on-Demand.
- Retailers such as Amazon, Barnes and Noble, Apple, Google, Bookstores and Libraries.
- eBooks, Audiobooks, Paperbacks, and Hardcovers.
- Keywords and Categories.
- Uploading your book to Amazon, Ingram Spark, and Draft2Digital.
- Launch Promotion.

- Amazon Advertising.
- Getting Reviews and Learning from Reviews.
- Amazon Algorithms.
- Social Media.
- Do you need an Author Web Site/Facebook Page?
- Overseas Markets and Translations.
- Blogs and Podcasts.

You may be sitting there thinking, I don't need to know anything about marketing or promotion; my publisher will look after all that. Well, stick around. You are in for a shock.

We will discuss the content and nature of your book idea, but by the same token, this book is not a course in creative writing.

Plenty of people can provide detailed instruction and critical feedback on your work, and it's certainly a good idea to find someone qualified, experienced, and capable to help you.

After all, there is always something to learn.

Chapter Four
How Traditional Publishing Works

TRADITIONAL PUBLISHERS SUCH as the Big Five - Penguin Random House, Simon and Schuster, Harper Collins, Macmillan, and Hachette have, for many years, worked with literary agents who represent authors and pitch their manuscripts to them.

All the same, some publishers will accept what they call unsolicited manuscripts, which are manuscripts that authors submit directly themselves.

- It can be just as difficult to secure an agent as it is a publisher (possibly more so), and an agent will charge you 15% of your royalty income as a commission if they secure you a publishing deal.

- They won't charge you anything upfront, but they will charge you a commission on any future royalty income.

- It may take you a year or two to find an agent (if you can get one at all), and if you do, it is likely to take another two or three years before your book is published. And that's if your agent can secure a publishing deal in the first place.

- Realistically, allow at least three to four years. And that is a best-case scenario.

- You can, of course, submit a manuscript to a publisher yourself.

- Be aware, however, that publishers will almost certainly only reply if they are curious. And that may take them a year or two. What's more, if they are interested and make you an offer, it will be at least another year or two before your book is published. Again, that is a best-case scenario.

- And if you get sick and tired of waiting and decide to publish that same book yourself (while publishers are supposedly still considering it), they will drop you like a hot rock.

- You may complete your manuscript, submit it to agents and publishers, and sit around for years before anything happens. If indeed it ever does, and the fact is it probably won't.

- That's no reflection on the quality of your writing; that's the reality. Agents and publishers get hundreds of submissions every day, and only a select few ever progress to publication.

- So let's say you do progress. Your publisher may pay you a modest advance of a couple of thousand dollars, but more likely no advance at all. And you will have to earn any advance back from future royalty income before earning anything more.

- An advance is not a sign-on fee or a bonus. It is just that, an advance. It will be paid in installments over a period of years, and in this day and age, advances are becoming increasingly rare, particularly for first-time authors.

- Your publisher will look after editing, proofreading, interior formatting, and cover design before producing Advance Reader Copies, which it will distribute to a select group of readers, libraries, book groups, and social media influencers. They will then monitor the interest these people generate in your book, and, needless to say, focus their efforts and marketing spend on the books that secure the most attention.

This process alone is likely to take at least twelve months.

- Your publisher may offer to pay you a royalty of between 5% and 8% of the retail price of your book, but be aware this will be calculated net of any local taxes and further reduced by various trade discounts, retailer returns, promotional pricing, and whatever else they can think of to reduce your income.

- After three to four years, you may earn $1.20 per paperback and $2.00 for an eBook, less a further 15% if you have an agent. What's more, most traditional publishers will only pay you twice a year, every six months.

I said earlier that you are in for a bit of a shock, and here it is.

- The two most prominent publishers in the world, namely Penguin Random House and Simon & Schuster, were recently involved in a major court case in the USA regarding whether their proposed merger breached America's anti-trust laws.

- During that case, senior executives from both companies presented the following figures under oath in court.

- These are not figures I sourced from the Internet. These are figures that were presented and recorded in an American court.

- Both companies combined will publish 58,000 titles across every genre each year, everything from spy thrillers to romance novels, children's books, and recipes.

- 50% - half of those books will sell fewer than a dozen copies.

- Of the remaining 50% of those books, 90% will sell fewer than 2,000 copies.

- 2,000 copies was presented in court as a financial 'break-even.'

Feel free to check my math, but I make that 58,000 books released by the world's largest and most successful publishers, with the best editors, dealing with the best literary agents, who knock back countless manuscript submissions every single day, and they fail 95% of the time.

If you intend submitting your manuscript to a traditional publisher, you might want to bear those numbers in mind, because if you were one of those publishers, where would you be devoting the majority, if not the entirety of your marketing resources and budget?

In fact, forget about the top 5%. Commercial publishers will focus most (if not all) of their marketing resources on a handful of bestsellers and reap all the profits they can from those few titles that break out and become hugely popular.

- These days, countless authors (who are traditionally published) find themselves coordinating and paying for their own advertising, promotion, and marketing for a fraction of the royalties they could be earning if they published their own books.

- Let's say a traditional publisher has published your book, and it's struggling to make any sales.

- If that's the case, your publisher will not devote any time, money, or resources to marketing it. They will be too busy putting all their time, money, and effort behind their latest literary sensation.

- And when you call them and ask what they are doing to promote your book, they will most likely say, "Well, what are you doing? Are you creating and posting content on social media? Are you advertising your book on Amazon? Are you contacting bloggers and podcasters? Are you speaking to book clubs and contacting social media influencers?"

- In short, your publisher will (almost certainly) expect you to do all those things and more to promote your book, and all so they can reap most of the profits and continue paying you your modest royalty.

- It is certainly challenging to secure a book deal with a traditional publisher, and even if you do, you still need to be part of that top 5% to get any sort of love and attention - if not the top 0.5%.

- Of course, one of the benefits of traditional publishing is that your book <u>may</u> be stocked in bookstores and be available from libraries.

- Your book will also be eligible to appear in Newspaper Bestseller Lists as such things are the sole domain of traditionally published books, as are the vast majority of literary awards.

- So, if those things matter to you, then you should definitely pursue a traditional publishing deal.

- By the same token, if you publish your own book and implement the distribution strategy that I outline in this book, your book will be available from bookstores and libraries all over the world, even though it probably won't be available in bookstores or libraries. At least not to begin with.

- For example, anyone could call into just about any bookstore, anywhere in the world, and ask for one of my books. They almost certainly won't have it in stock, but they can look it up on a computer in a matter of seconds, order a copy, and have it in a few days. It's the same deal with libraries.

- When I presented this information to a friend of a friend, who is a journalist and author herself, she remarked, "Well, yes, but there is a certain cachet in being traditionally published." I responded, "What will cachet buy you?"

If you intend to submit your work to traditional publishers or literary agents (exclusively), you can still benefit from reading this book. Be aware, however, that it is tremendously difficult for any first-time author (in particular) to secure a traditional publishing deal if you are not already an established writer, celebrity, sports star, or social media influencer.

Don't be discouraged by that. It may be difficult, but it is not impossible, which is to say nothing of the fact I genuinely believe that you are better off publishing your own work rather than assigning the rights to your book to a traditional publisher. That may not have been the case ten years ago, but it is today.

If you intend to pitch your book to a publisher or literary agent, then here is a list of things to consider:

- First and foremost, do your research. Find out which publishers publish books like yours and which agents represent authors who produce similar books.

- There is no point pitching your science fiction novel or your children's book to publishers that don't publish books of that nature.

- Publishers and, to a lesser extent, literary agents will outline their submission criteria on their websites.

- If you do decide to submit your book, make sure you follow their instructions exactly.

- If they ask for the first three chapters of your book, together with a synopsis and a cover letter, give them precisely that. Don't send four chapters and no synopsis.

- Similarly, if they ask for a sample chapter, send them your best one, and on the day they accept manuscript submissions. A while back, Macmillan accepted submissions by email on the first Friday of each month between 10.00 am and 4.00 pm. That may have changed since, so be sure to check.

- If you submit your manuscript outside of their specified window or in a manner that doesn't comply with their particular guidelines, it will almost certainly go in the trash folder.

- Publishers and agents will want to know if there is a market for your book, why you are the best person to write it, why you are an expert authority, for example, and why your book will be an enormous commercial success. So tell them all that in a cover letter/email.

- Have you been published previously? How successful are you already? Are you hugely famous with a massive social media following?

- Publishers won't consider your book because you are polite, friendly, and nice, although this can only help. They may consider your book if they think it can be a commercial success.

Chapter Five
The Retail Book Market

TO GIVE YOU an idea of just how competitive the retail book market is, consider this;

70% of all books sold worldwide are sold on Amazon. Not just eBooks, not just paperbacks or audiobooks, and not just online sales. That's all books. Including books sold by physical bookstores and other online retailers.

Amazon is the measuring stick. It is far and above the world's most significant book retailer, and it has more than twelve million English-language book titles published on its platform.

You may be sitting there thinking, I don't buy books from Amazon. I don't like Amazon, and you know what? Many people don't, but you'll find that most people search for books on Amazon and find books on Amazon, even if they buy those same books elsewhere.

Amazon is where everyone is, every book, every author, and every publisher, while its search engine algorithms are unsurpassed.

The reason Amazon is so successful is because it has the unique capacity to put the right products in front of the right people at the right time, better than anyone else.

Amazon is Not a Bookstore.

It is a Search Engine.

If you are serious about selling your book (online or in bookstores) you must focus your attention on Amazon, and do all you can to help people discover and find your book on Amazon. Everything else will follow from that.

The World's Top Ten Retail Book Markets

1. United States
2. China
3. Germany
4. Japan
5. France
6. UK
7. Italy
8. Spain
9. India
10. Brazil

The United States is the world's largest retail book market; it accounts for 55% of the world's English-language book sales and more than 33% overall.

Chapter Six

The Four Pillars of Successful Book Publishing

CONSIDER THESE PILLARS the four legs of a very tall platform that you will climb up and stand on top of to launch your book into the world.

Now imagine if just one of those pillars is weak, flimsy, broken, or missing.

What will happen when you stand on top of it to hurl your book into the marketplace with all the force and energy you can muster?

The whole thing will collapse, you will fall flat on your face, and the entire exercise will prove both painful and expensive.

If you like, think of these same elements as the four wheels of a car.

You might have a brand-new Ferrari purring away in the garage. But if one of the tires is flat, you're not going anywhere.

All four of these elements need to be in the best possible shape they can be if you are going to succeed. Three out of four will not get the job done.

Happily, these four elements are very easy to remember, as they can be defined thus;

A B C D

A - Audience

- Books sell by word of mouth. Always have, always will.

- You need to know exactly who your audience is and write a book that will appeal to your audience - a book your audience will love. That way, people can read your book, enjoy your book, and tell other people about your book.

- As you write, even as you plan and outline your book, always write to entertain and engage your audience - your target reader.

- You must always keep your target reader in mind, because your reader is always thinking, "What's in this for me?"

- Readers don't care if you have sold one copy of your book or one million. They don't know you, and for the most part, they don't care about you. But you want them to part with their hard-earned cash to buy your book.

- When you first publish your book, you will have at least twenty copies printed and delivered. You will open the box they came in, take a copy out, and hold it in your hands. You will stare at it and delight in the fact your name appears on the cover and spine. And you should feel very proud as you enact this whole process, but never forget who you are writing this book for.

- You are not writing this book for yourself, and you are not writing it for the benefit of your friends and family.

- You are writing this book to appeal to your target reader, your audience, which is why you need to allocate your book to the correct categories and associate it with the most relevant search term keywords when you publish it on Amazon (and with other platforms) so that you get your book in front of the right people.

- If you can sell a hundred copies of your book to your target audience (people who are going to read it and love it) and each of those people (on average) tell ten people, who tell ten people, who tell ten people - that's how you sell a million books.

- You do not sell a million books by advertising on Facebook.

B - Book

- Writing a great book is no guarantee of success. Writing a great book is the price of admission.

- You need to write a book that your audience will love and that they will tell other people about. It doesn't have to be a great book from my point of view. It needs to be a great book from the perspective of your audience.

- No one has ever written a book that appeals to everyone, and no one ever will, and before you shout out, "Harry Potter," I have never bought a Harry Potter book, never read a Harry Potter book, and never even picked one up.

- Did you know that J.K. Rowling's literary agent pitched her first manuscript to more than a dozen publishers in the UK before one of them made an offer to publish it?

- And why do you think that happened?

- Because the people considering the manuscript (if they bothered to read it at all) were most likely forty-something graduates from Oxford and Cambridge who were never the book's audience in the first place.

- Imagine, if just one of those people had the sense and the initiative to give that manuscript to their twelve-year-old niece or nephew. They might not have missed out on the most significant publishing phenomenon of the 21st century.

C - Cover

- It may surprise you to know that the job of your book cover is not to sell your book.

- The job of your book cover is to catch people's attention, pique their interest, and spark their curiosity, so they click on it and go to your book's Detail Page, where they can read your Book Description, any reviews and consider the price.

- The first time anyone sees your book cover, will almost certainly be online, amongst several other results from a keyword or category search on Amazon.

- Even if someone enters the title of your book, together with your author name, your book cover will still appear with fifteen or more others on a page of search results. And the last thing you can afford at this, or any stage, is for your book cover to appear less interesting, less relevant, and less engaging than another.

- The book cover images displayed in Amazon search results are called thumbnails, and they are called thumbnails for a reason.

- Most people search for books on mobile devices, even if they ultimately buy those books on a desktop, and in this instance, the size of your book cover is about the size of the nail on your little finger.

- In short, your book cover and its title must be striking, relevant, and they must stand out.

- Nothing screams third-rate self-published more than a second-rate cover.

- Your book cover can't just be good, and it can't just be great. It must be outstanding.

- Book covers, together with titles and subtitles, are hugely important.

- You have over twelve million English language competitors on Amazon alone, and books with second-rate covers invariably fail. They don't just struggle. They fail.

Distributors like Amazon and Ingram Spark offer Cover Creation Tools on their websites, where you can design your own book cover.

You can enter the exterior dimensions of your book, then enter a page count (which will define the spine width), and thereafter upload a royalty-free image that you downloaded from websites like Shutterstock or Deposit Photos, before entering your book's title and author name, as you scroll through a myriad of different typefaces, styles, and effects.

This whole process has no end of possibilities, so let me break down Book Cover Design for you to Three Golden Rules.

If you follow each of these three rules, I am confident that you will achieve an excellent outcome with the design of your book cover.

Golden Rules of Book Cover Design

1. **Don't Do It Yourself.**
   - Under no circumstances whatsoever should you even consider designing your own book cover.

2. **Don't Use Someone on Fiverr, Upwork, 99Designs, or your Best Friend's Niece because she's a Graphic Designer.**

3. **Always Work with an Experienced, Professional, Specialist Book Cover Designer.**

- Present your designer with a very clear and detailed brief of precisely what your book is about, together with the sort of people it is written for - your audience, in other words.

- Include the book's title and subtitle, key elements or themes, and a description of your main character, if that's appropriate.

- Include links to other book covers that you admire, and to other covers that your book will be competing with.

- Give your cover designer all the relevant information that you can, but don't design the cover for them.

Several years ago (having already published my first novel), I was reading a book about self-publishing that had an entire chapter devoted to cover design.

The author made some excellent and very interesting points.

Among them was the fact that readers have certain expectations when it comes to the book covers that occupy specific genres. Readers expect covers in a particular genre to have a specific look. Romance covers all look the same; science fiction books have a similar appearance, as do murder mysteries and spy thrillers.

As I read this chapter, I saw a sentence at the bottom of a page that read;

A lot of authors think to themselves – "All the covers in my book's genre look the same. I'm going to do something different. I'm going to stand out."

As I considered that passage, I thought to myself, "That's exactly what I did!" and feeling very pleased and proud of myself, I turned the page to see the following sentence read;

This is a really bad idea.

By all means stand out. Just don't be different.

These days, I work with a team of experienced, professional, specialist book cover designers called Damonza.

Damonza is owned and operated by a fellow called Damon Freeman. He is based in Auckland, New Zealand, and I believe he has a small network of designers around the world with whom he works.

Damonza only design book covers. They don't design logos, posters, or websites. They only design book covers. They create book covers for major publishers, and they design them for self-published authors. They make no distinction.

They are not cheap, but they are very, very good.

Damonza Book Cover Design:

Trends evolve in book cover design, colors and typefaces come in and out of favor, while an almost imperceptible change to the design of a book's cover can make a tremendous difference to its commercial appeal.

A few years ago, I read a study of how one publisher did a 'split test' with two different covers for the same spy thriller novel.

- At first glance, both covers looked the same. The only difference was that on one cover (in the distance), a small, dark, shadowy figure was running toward the camera. On the other cover, that small, dark, shadowy figure was running away from the camera.

- The small, dark, shadowy figure was the same size in each instance, and everything else was identical; title, typeface, author name, and so on.

- In one cover design, the small, dark, shadowy figure was running toward the camera, and in the other, the figure was running away from the camera.

- The book cover was eight and a half inches deep, and the small, dark, shadowy figure was, at best, an inch and a half high.

- The difference between the two book covers was almost imperceptible.

- Yet, the book with a cover showing the figure running away from the camera outsold the book with the figure running toward the camera by a ratio greater than 10 to 1.

- Experienced, professional, specialist book cover designers know this sort of thing.

A great cover design starts with a great brief, so when you present your designer with the details of your book, don't just include the title, subtitle, and author name. Tell them precisely what your book's audience is and exactly the sort of message that you want your cover to convey.

If you choose to work with a traditional publisher, you will need to compromise regarding cover design because it is your publisher that holds the rights to your book. Although they may consult you to some degree, in the design process, the ultimate decision will be theirs to make, not yours.

Above all though, appreciate this;

Book Cover Design is an Investment, Not an Expense.

D - Description

- Your Book Description is the most crucial element in your entire marketing and promotion strategy.

- Your Book Description will appear on your book's Detail Page with Amazon, and it is akin to the copy that might appear on the back cover of your book when someone takes it off a shelf in a bookstore. In fact, your book's Detail Page effectively replicates that process.

- Always remember that your Book Description is Sales Copy, and it is this element that needs to convert browsers into buyers.

- Everything else you do, from identifying an audience, to writing a great book, designing an outstanding cover, researching keywords and categories, advertising, getting reviews, and generating interest from bloggers, podcasters, and social media influencers; all that will ever do is generate traffic to your book's Detail Page, where people can read your Book Description, look at your reviews and consider the price of your book, before deciding whether or not to buy it.

- You simply cannot afford to present people with a Book Description that leaves them thinking (at any point),

"Meh," because they will click away in less than a second and never return.

- All of the hard work, effort, and expense involved in getting people to visit your book's Detail Page in the first place will amount to nothing if you don't have a compelling Book Description that converts browsers into buyers.

- It's like putting a full-page ad in the newspaper and having thousands of people walk into your store the next day, only to walk out again without buying anything.

Golden Rules of a Great Book Description

- Think like a reader - not an author.

- Always include a headline in **Bold Type** (Upper and Lower Case).

- The headline must be relevant to your book and spark curiosity/interest and/or what's at stake. It may take the form of a question.

- 150 to 200 words, including the headline.

- Write short paragraphs with no more than two sentences each. Ideally one.

- Never present people with a large block of text. That's a massive turn-off.

- If possible and feasible, compare your book to other successful titles and authors.

- Don't just tell people what your book is about. Tell them how they will benefit from reading it.

- Don't be modest. Remember, you, as the author, are not writing this copy. Your publisher is.

- Speak one-on-one with your customer and use words like you, you are, and your.

- Always finish with a Call to Action, such as - Get your copy of (name of book) today. It's important that you tell people what to do.

From my book Positively Pazzo

Beyond the Classroom: How Italian Lessons Changed Everything

When fifty-five-year-old Michael Francis joins an Italian for Beginners class, he has no idea that classroom chaos is the prelude to a grand adventure.

Armed with unwavering optimism and a tendency to conjugate verbs in all the wrong tenses, he flies to Italy and travels across the country that has captured his imagination.

From hilarious interactions with street food vendors to terrifying mountain bus journeys, his many misadventures demonstrate that sometimes the best stories start with getting everything wrong.

For readers who enjoyed Bill Bryson's *Neither Here Nor There* or Frances Mayes' *Under the Tuscan Sun*, *Positively Pazzo* offers a refreshing twist on the traditional travel memoir.

This heartwarming tale isn't just about learning a language. It's about a man who realizes it's never too late to become a beginner again.

Pick up your copy of *Positively Pazzo* today and discover how one man's quest to learn Italian became an unexpected journey of self-discovery, proving that the most valuable souvenirs are not found in gift shops but in the memories we bring home.

What is the Purpose of Your Book Description?

And don't say, "To sell my book," because Amazon sells your book, bookstores and other online retailers sell your book. You publish your book. Other people sell it for you.

> The Purpose of your Book Description is to Persuade People to Buy your Book.

- This is where the rubber hits the road. It's not even accurate or correct to describe it as a description or, worse, a blurb.

- It is Sales Copy.

- You want people to read your Book Description and think to themselves, "Wow! This sounds great. I have got to buy this book. This is just the sort of thing I'm looking for."

- There is no point in identifying an audience and writing a great book with an outstanding cover, to say nothing of advertising it on Amazon and engaging with people on social media if your Book Description isn't absolutely first-rate.

In the past, I have written (what I thought were) tremendous Book Bescriptions, only to spend a lot of money on Amazon ads that demonstrated people were clicking on my book covers and looking at my book Detail Pages but not buying my books.

I can't tell you how disheartening that is.

It's one thing for people not to buy your book. Still, when you pay hundreds of dollars every month just to give people the opportunity not to buy it, it's a very bitter pill to swallow.

Your Book Description must convert browsers into buyers.

Now, I dare say there any number of people, in the world today, who are perfectly capable of writing a great book, and a really great Book Description.

Apparently, I'm not one of them.

However, I discovered a tremendous artificial intelligence program that has helped me no end when it comes to writing my Book Descriptions.

It's called Claude AI.

- Claude AI

I suggest you write the best Book Description you can, and after outlining a clearly defined audience, enter that information and your Book Description into the Claude AI website, asking it to improve it.

I think it's a good idea to tackle the headline separately.

Claude AI is a fantastic asset in developing Book Descriptions, and it's free - at least for a few daily interactions anyway.

I am not suggesting that you simply accept whatever Claude presents you with, but certainly, use it as a template and a source of ideas. You can always construct a description using some of the elements that Claude has suggested, together with your own copy, and enter it again.

I usually achieve the outcome that I am looking for after five or six interactions.

You have undoubtedly heard of ChatGPT - the great poster child of artificial intelligence.

By all means, try it out with your Book Description. In my experience, it pales by comparison.

Some points to remember:

- The headline of your Book Description is hugely important.

- Many people never get past the headline, and the battle is lost if you haven't caught their attention and sparked their curiosity at this point.

- You may find a compelling headline buried in the text of your Book Description. If so, take it out and amend that particular section.

- I suggest you write several headlines and give them and your Book Description an 'overnight test.'

- An overnight test means putting them aside and looking at them again (with fresh eyes) the next day.

- Some of the copy or headlines you wrote, and thought were tremendous the previous day, may not measure up quite so well a few hours later.

- When you are happy with your Book Description, check the effectiveness of your headline with the AMI Headline Analyzer.

- AMI Headline Analyzer:

- This free AI tool will give you a percentage score analysis for your headline. The higher the score, the more effective it considers your headline to be.

- I wouldn't trust it unconditionally, but it's a worthwhile and interesting exercise.

- Also, check your headline ideas with family and friends, but give them a list to choose from. If you only present them with one idea, they will just say it's great.

- Once you are happy with your Book Description and you are ready to publish your book on Amazon, you need to have your Book Description formatted in HTML code, so that it appears as neat and concise as possible, with the headline in bold, paragraphs all neatly spaced, and any lists featuring bullet points or numbers.

- To do this, paste your Book Description (Ctrl + V) into the FREE Kindlepreneur Book Description Generator.

  - Kindlepreneur Book Description Generator:

Now you can create a headline - H4, highlight any book titles (including your own) in *italics* and format any lists with bullet points or numbers.

Once you are happy, click 'Generate My Code,' then copy and save your newly formatted Book Description as a Word file.

Later, you will paste this code into your book Set-Up Pages on Amazon KDP.

Chapter Seven
Your Book Idea

IF YOU ARE not familiar with the concept of an Elevator Pitch, I will explain it.

Imagine you have an appointment in a multi-story office building.

When you step into the elevator on the first floor, you see that someone is already there - no doubt a resident of the building who has parked their car in the basement.

Then you realize that the other person in the elevator is, in fact, the President of Fat Cat Publishing International, who has an office on the sixth floor.

You seize the chance to tell her about your book.

"I'm sorry to trouble you," you say, "But I have a book idea I would love to tell you about?"

"Really?" she replies, "What's your book about?"

You now have whatever time it takes for the elevator to reach the sixth floor to present her with an outline of your book, without wasting her time explaining any ideas or themes you are still working through.

So do that now. Outline your book in fewer than ten words.

If it were me:

<u>Positively Pazzo</u>

Fifty-Five-Year-Old Man Decides to Learn Italian.

<u>Yards and Stripes</u>

Clumsy New Yorker Starts a Gardening Business in Connecticut.

Or perhaps something more familiar:

<u>Rocky</u>

Down and Out Fighter Gets One Last Shot.

This exercise aims to narrow your focus and it will prove particularly valuable shortly, when we discuss finding relevant search term keywords for your book.

Writing Visually

- We all learn to read books as children by looking at pictures.

- That doesn't change as we get older. We just create those same images in our minds.

- What we, as authors, need to do is to paint a picture in the minds of our readers.

- To do this, you need to write in your own voice, or the voice of you main character if they are telling the story.

- Type the words on the screen or write them on a page as you would say them, as if you were telling the story to a friend.

- You are not writing a letter or sending someone an email, you are speaking to them.

- Try recording yourself telling the story. That may help.

One of the nicest compliments people who have read my books have paid me is they can hear my voice in their heads as they read the words on the page.

- Many people fall into the trap of thinking they need to use lots of big words and elaborate language to make a story interesting and entertaining.

- That's simply not the case. In fact, if anything, the reverse is true.

- If you want your book to have commercial appeal and reach as large an audience as possible, write a story using the sort of words you use every day.

- Avoid complicated similes and elaborate adjectives. There is no benefit in showing off how clever you are.

- The bigger the words you use and the more complicated your language, the smaller your audience will become.

- This approach has worked for some of the most successful authors in the world, and it will work for you.

- Paint a colorful, interesting picture using clear, straightforward language, and you will appeal to a larger audience and possibly to a traditional publisher.

- You won't connect with a reader and establish any sort of rapport if you use words they don't understand.

Almost thirty years ago, I had just finished writing my first novel when I rang a Writer's Centre in Brooklyn, hoping to solicit some advice about getting it published.

A very pretentious woman I spoke to said, "Well, you must understand it is very, very difficult to get a book published." Then she added, "Is yours a literary work?"

At the time, I didn't even know what that meant, and I was holding the phone, thinking, "Well, it's a book, I don't know."

Then she added (with some disdain), "Or more commercial?"

"Oh, commercial," I said.

She replied, "Well, perhaps not quite so difficult then."

Chapter Eight
How to Write a Novel

WRITING A NOVEL can feel overwhelming. With countless books offering complex formulas and intricate plot structures, many aspiring novelists find themselves weighed down before they even begin. But here's the truth; every great novel, regardless of genre or length, rests on three fundamental pillars that readers instinctively crave.

These three elements form the backbone of every story that has ever kept a reader turning pages late into the night. Master these, and you will have the foundation for a novel that your audience will want to read.

The Three Pillars of Novel Writing

Every compelling novel answers three crucial questions:

1. **Character:** Who are they?

2. **Conflict:** What do they want?

3. **Stakes:** What will happen if they don't get it?

These aren't just writing techniques - they are the DNA of human storytelling. If you can answer these three questions clearly and compellingly, you have the roadmap for your entire novel.

Pillar One: Character - Who Are They?

Your protagonist isn't just a name on a page or a collection of physical attributes. They are the beating heart of your story, and readers will only care about what happens if they first care about who it's happening to.

Creating a Three-Dimensional Character

- **The Surface Level:** This is what readers see first - age, appearance, occupation, and social status. But don't stop here. Many aspiring novelists make the mistake of thinking a detailed physical description creates a compelling character. It doesn't.

- **The Emotional Core:** What drives your character emotionally? What are their deepest fears, strongest desires, and most painful memories? This emotional landscape will inform every decision they make throughout your novel.

- **The Hidden Wound:** Every compelling protagonist carries a broken piece inside them - a wound from their past that shapes how they perceive the world. This wound will be tested and, ideally, healed through the events of your story.

The Character Arc Framework

Your protagonist needs to change over the course of your novel. They cannot be the same person on page 300 that they were on page 1.

This transformation happens in three stages:

- **Who they are at the beginning** - shaped by their wound and limiting beliefs.

- **What forces them to change** - the conflict and challenges you put them through.

- **Who they become by the end** - having grown beyond their original limitations.

Supporting Characters That Matter

Every character in your novel should serve the story.

Secondary characters aren't just there to populate your fictional world - they are there to reveal different aspects of your protagonist and to create or complicate the central conflict.

Ask yourself: "How does this character challenge, support, or reveal something important about my protagonist?"

If you can't answer this question, consider whether that character belongs in your story.

Pillar Two: Conflict - What Do They Want?

Conflict isn't just arguments or fight scenes. Conflict is the engine that drives your story forward. It's the gap between what your protagonist wants and what stands in their way.

The Hierarchy of Want

Effective novels operate on multiple levels of desire:

- **Surface Want:** What your protagonist thinks they want at the beginning of the story. This is often external and tangible - such as a relationship, revenge, or escape.

- **Deep Need:** What your protagonist actually needs to become whole. This is usually internal and tied to healing their wound or overcoming their flaw. Often, the protagonist doesn't recognize this need until later in the story.

- **The Contradiction:** The most compelling novels create a situation where getting what the protagonist wants might prevent them from getting what they need, or vice versa.

Types of Conflict to Layer into Your Story

- **Internal Conflict:** The war within your protagonist - their fears, doubts, moral dilemmas, and competing desires. This is often the most critical conflict because it's what creates the character arc.

- **Interpersonal Conflict:** Conflicts with other characters - family, friends, enemies, lovers. These relationships should force your protagonist to confront their internal conflicts.

- **Societal Conflict:** Your protagonist versus the rules, expectations, or systems of their world. This can range from a dystopian government to something as intimate as family expectations.

- **Environmental Conflict:** Physical challenges that test your protagonist - natural disasters, survival situations, or any external obstacle that requires them to act.

The Escalation Principle

Conflict must escalate throughout your novel. Each obstacle your protagonist overcomes should lead to a bigger challenge. Each victory should cost them something. Each defeat should raise the stakes for their next attempt.

Think of conflict as a pressure cooker. You are constantly turning up the heat, adding more pressure, until something has to give in the climax.

Practical Exercise: Mapping the Want

Create a conflict map for your protagonist:

- What do they want at the beginning?

- What's stopping them from getting it?

- What do they think will happen if they do get it?

- What will actually happen if they get it?

- What do they really need instead?

- What's stopping them from recognizing this need?

Pillar Three: Stakes - What Will Happen If They Don't Get It?

Stakes are what make readers care. They transform a series of events into a story that matters. Without clear stakes, readers have no reason to worry about your protagonist or keep turning pages.

The Four Levels of Stakes

- **Personal Stakes:** What will your protagonist lose personally if they fail? This could be their life, their identity, their self-respect, or their relationships.

- **Emotional Stakes:** What emotional consequences will failure bring? Heartbreak, guilt, regret, or the loss of hope itself.

- **Moral Stakes:** What principles or values are at risk? Will your protagonist compromise their integrity? Will evil triumph over good?

- **Universal Stakes:** What larger consequences extend beyond your protagonist? Will others suffer? Will the world change for the worse?

The most compelling novels operate on multiple levels simultaneously. Your protagonist might be fighting to save their marriage (personal), prove they're not a coward (emotional), maintain their principles (moral), and protect their community (universal).

Making Stakes Feel Real

Stakes are only effective if readers believe them.

Therefore;

- **Establish them early**: Readers need to understand what's at risk before they're invested in the outcome.

- **Make them specific:** "Everything will be ruined" is less compelling than "She'll lose custody of her daughter and have to start over in a new city where nobody knows her name."

- **Increase them gradually:** As your story progresses, the stakes should grow larger and more personal.

- **Make failure a real possibility:** If readers don't believe your protagonist could actually fail, there's no tension.

The Ticking Clock

One of the most effective ways to heighten stakes is to add time pressure. This could be:

- **A literal deadline** - the bomb explodes at midnight.

- **A natural progression** - the disease gets worse each day.

- **Social pressure** - the wedding is in three weeks.

- **An emotional urgency** - before she changes her mind.

Time pressure forces your protagonist to act, prevents them from endless deliberation, and keeps readers engaged.

Practical Exercise: Stakes Assessment

For each major scene in your novel, identify:

- What is your protagonist trying to accomplish?

- What will happen if they succeed?

- What will happen if they fail?

- Why should the reader care about either outcome?

If you can't answer these questions, you may need to raise the stakes or clarify the conflict.

Bringing the Three Pillars Together

These three elements don't work in isolation - they are interconnected and should reinforce each other throughout your novel.

The Opening Pages

Your first chapter should introduce all three pillars:

- Give readers a clear sense of who your protagonist is.

- Hint at what they want or what they're struggling with.

- Suggest what's at stake if they don't resolve their situation.

You don't need to explain everything immediately. Still, readers should sense that something important is happening to someone they are beginning to care about.

The Middle Pages

The bulk of your novel will test and develop these three elements:

- Your protagonist will face increasingly difficult obstacles in pursuit of their goal.

- Each challenge will reveal more about who they are and force them to grow.

- The stakes will escalate, making failure increasingly costly.

The Climax

Your climax should bring all these elements to a head:

- Your protagonist faces their greatest challenge.

- Everything they want hangs in the balance.

- The stakes reach their highest point.

- The outcome will determine who they become.

The Resolution

Your ending should show how the three pillars have resolved:

- Who your protagonist has become throughout their journey.

- Whether they achieved what they wanted or discovered what they needed.

- How the stakes have been resolved and what it has cost them.

Common Mistakes to Avoid

- **A Passive Protagonist:** If your protagonist isn't actively pursuing their goal, readers will lose interest. Things can't just happen to them - they must make choices and take action.

- **Stakes That Don't Matter:** If the consequences of failure aren't meaningful to your protagonist or your readers, the story lacks urgency.

- **Conflict Without Growth:** If your protagonist faces obstacles but doesn't change or learn, you have a series of events, not a story.

- **Characters Who Want Nothing:** A protagonist without a clear desire is a protagonist readers won't follow.

Your Novel Writing Action Plan

1. **Start with Character:** Before plotting any scenes or worrying about structure, get to know your protagonist inside and out. What drives them? What do they believe about the world? How will they change?

2. **Clarify the Want:** Be specific about what your protagonist desires and why.

Make sure this want is strong enough to drive an entire novel.

3. **Raise the Stakes:** Determine what your protagonist will lose if they fail. Ensure readers will care about these consequences.

4. **Test and Escalate:** Put your protagonist through increasingly complex challenges that test their character and raise the stakes.

5. **Force Growth:** Make sure your protagonist can't achieve their goal without changing who they are.

Key Elements to Keep Top-of-Mind

- Readers don't care about your plot - they care about your people.

- They don't worry about your twists - they worry about your characters.

- They won't remember your clever dialogue - they will remember how your story made them feel.

Build your Novel on These Three Solid Pillars

- A character worth caring about.

- A conflict worth following.

- Stakes worth worrying about.

Do this, and you will create the foundation for a story that readers won't be able to put down.

Your novel's appeal isn't defined by how complex your plot is or how beautiful your prose sounds. It's determined by how much readers care about what happens to the person at the center of your story.

Make them care about your main character, show them what your character wants, and convince them that failure will matter.

Chapter Nine
How to Write a Memoir

WHILE FICTION SALES have remained relatively flat, memoir sales have surged by 35% over the past five years.

Readers are hungry for authentic, transformational stories that offer both entertainment and insight.

Most bestselling memoirs cover a specific period of time or focus on particular relationships, rather than presenting a comprehensive coverage of someone's life.

- **Time-focused memoirs** concentrate on a specific period when a significant change occurred. This approach works well if you experienced a dramatic transformation during a defined timeframe - for example, addiction recovery, career transition, or a relationship change.

- **Relationship-focused memoirs** delve into your connection with specific individuals who have shaped your development. These might focus on parents, spouses, children, mentors, or even adversaries. The relationship becomes the lens through which you explore broader themes of love, family, growth, or conflict.

- **Challenge-focused memoirs** may present specific obstacles that you overcame. Such stories work well when you have been challenged by illness, discrimination, or poverty.

Structuring Your Memoir

- **A thematic structure** organizes chapters around different aspects of your central theme, rather than a clearly defined timeline. Suppose your memoir explores how childhood trauma shaped your adult relationships. In that case, you might present chapters that explore different relationships with family, friends, romantic partners, or work colleagues, illustrating how the same underlying patterns emerge in various contexts.

- **A circular structure** begins with a pivotal moment, then moves backward to show how you arrived at that point, and then forward to reveal the consequences. This structure can work well if your memoir focuses on a specific decision, a crisis, or a realization that serves as a natural focal point.

- **A braided structure** alternates between different time periods or storylines that eventually converge. This approach works when your memoir involves parallel narratives - perhaps alternating between your story and a parent's story or between past and present perspectives of the same events.

- **A seasonal structure** is organized around natural rhythms (seasons, years, stages of life) when those cycles relate meaningfully to your theme. This structure works particularly well for memoirs about grief, recovery, parenting, or other experiences that involve a natural progression of events.

- Whatever structure you choose, create an outline that serves your theme rather than simply following a timeline.

- Each chapter should advance your central recollection about life, relationships, growth, or whatever universal truth your memoir explores.

Create Compelling Scenes

Memoir succeeds through scene construction, just as fiction does. Readers want to experience your story, not just learn about it. This means showing, not telling.

Be sure to use dialogue, setting, and sensory details to recreate important moments rather than simply summarizing them.

Dialogue reconstruction in memoir requires balancing accuracy with readability. You can't be expected to remember exact conversations from years ago, but you can recreate the essence of essential exchanges. Focus on capturing the emotional truth and speech patterns of the people involved, rather than worrying about absolute accuracy.

When reconstructing dialogue, consider what you remember most clearly. It might be an emotional impact or the surprising things people said - the moments that revealed their character. Build dialogue around these elements while staying true to how people spoke. If your father always used specific phrases or your mother had distinctive speech patterns, incorporate those details into your narrative. This will make your dialogue authentic.

The setting and atmosphere will absorb readers in your experience. Don't just tell readers that you grew up poor. Show them the apartment with its thin walls, where you could hear neighbors arguing. Show them the refrigerator that hummed so loudly because the motor was dying, and how you had to step over the loose floorboards that creaked and shifted as you walked on them. Specific sensory details will make your experience more vivid and relatable.

Balance Reflection and Action

Too much action without reflection leaves readers entertained but unchanged.

- Too much reflection without action bores readers with philosophical musing.

- The most engaging memoirs weave together scenes and insight, letting readers experience events while understanding their significance.

Consider this Approach

- Write the scene first - focusing on recreating what happened as vividly as possible.

- Then, add a reflection, one that explains why these events mattered, what they taught you, and how they connect to your memoir's larger themes.

- This ensures that you will present readers with both an entertaining narrative and meaningful insights.

Finding Your Own Voice

Your memoir voice will differ from your fiction voice because readers know they are encountering a real person rather than a constructed narrator. Your memoir voice should feel and sound like your conversational self - more focused than casual speech, but recognizably you.

An age-appropriate voice becomes crucial when writing about your childhood or adolescent experiences. In this instance, you have a choice; write from your current adult perspective looking back or attempt to recreate your younger self. Most successful memoirs employ an adult perspective because it allows for an insight and a context that your younger self couldn't provide.

However, you can still capture the emotional authenticity of younger experiences while writing from an adult perspective. Instead of - "When I was eight, I couldn't understand why my father was always angry," you might write - "At the age of eight, I could chart my father's anger as if I was tracking a storm - the low rumble of thunder that meant he'd had a difficult day, the sharp crack of lightning that sent me to my room, and the long silences that felt more dangerous than shouting."

Voice consistency throughout your memoir means establishing your narrative personality early on and maintaining it throughout.

- Are you naturally funny or serious?

- Analytical or intuitive?

- Optimistic or skeptical?

These traits should remain consistent even as you write about different periods of your life or varying emotional experiences.

Develop voice consistency by reading your favorite memoirs and analyzing how authors maintain their personalities while writing about diverse experiences.

Character Development in Real Life

Writing about real people presents unique challenges.

You need to create compelling, three-dimensional characters while remaining fair to people who may read your book and have their own perspectives on shared experiences.

- Portraying real people fairly doesn't mean portraying them in a positive light - it means portraying them honestly and accurately.

- Even difficult people in your life had redeeming qualities, and even people you loved had flaws.

- Readers trust narrators who present complex, realistic characters rather than portraying them as saints or villains.

When writing about someone who hurt you, focus on their behavior and the impact it had rather than character assassination. Instead of writing - "My mother was a narcissist who never cared about anyone but herself," describe specific incidents that demonstrate her selfish behavior and explain how it affected you. Let readers draw their own conclusions about her character while you focus on storytelling.

Creating composite characters can solve problems when you need to protect people's privacy or simplify your narrative. You might combine several similar people into one character or disguise someone's identity by changing identifiable details while keeping the essential relationship dynamics intact.

You can always disclose the composition of any such characters in an Author's Note at the end of your book.

Legal considerations of character portrayal require an understanding of fundamental defamation law. You can write truthfully about your own experiences, but avoid making statements about other people's motivations, any private behavior you didn't actually witness, or any accusations you can't prove.

When in doubt, focus on your experience and your response rather than on other people's character or actions.

Truth, Memory, and Creative License

Memoir exists in a space between journalism and fiction.

- Readers expect emotional honesty and factual accuracy where possible. Still, they understand that memory is imperfect and that storytelling sometimes requires a compression or reorganization of events.

- When your memory conflicts with documented evidence, or when other people remember events differently, prioritize the emotional truth while acknowledging your uncertainty. You might write - "I remember the argument lasting for hours, though it could have been minutes. "Grief has its own relationship with time," or "My sister remembers this differently, but in my memory, our mother's face showed disappointment rather than anger."

- Handling uncertain memories honestly will build trust with your reader. Acknowledge when you are unsure about any details while focusing on what you remember most clearly. This typically encompasses the emotional impact and essential facts of important events. Use phrases like, "I think," "as I remember it," or "it seemed to me" when appropriate.

- Fact-checking your own life involves gathering any available documentation - photos, letters, diaries, medical records and consulting with family members or friends who shared your experiences. Don't let minor factual uncertainties prevent you from telling important stories, but verify significant facts wherever possible.

- Gathering documents and records will enhance the accuracy of your memoir and inspire previously forgotten details.

- Old photos often evoke vivid memories of long-forgotten events, relationships, and emotions. Letters reveal how you thought and felt at the time, rather than how you remember thinking and feeling. Even mundane documents, such as medical records, can provide concrete details that ground your narrative in reality.

- Family members and old friends may remember events differently from you, and these differences can enrich your understanding of what happened. Approach interviews as information-gathering exercises rather than fact-verification.

Prepare Open-Ended Questions

- "What do you remember about that time when..."

- "How did you feel when..."

- "Did this specific thing happen?"

Record interviews wherever possible, and always ask permission before using someone's memories in your memoir.

Dealing with Emotional Content

Writing about trauma, loss, or conflict can trigger unexpected emotional responses.

- Plan for this by scheduling difficult chapters when you have emotional support available and fewer external demands.

- Consider writing the hardest chapters in short sessions rather than attempting to push through painful material.

- Some writers find it helpful to write emotional scenes quickly without editing, then return later when they have more emotional distance. Others prefer to write slowly and process emotions as they arise.

- Writing difficult memories may require professional support. If writing your memoir triggers feelings of depression, anxiety or any other mental health concerns, consider working with a therapist who is familiar with the creative process.

- Writing a memoir can be healing, but it should never replace professional treatment for severe trauma.

Maintaining Momentum

Every memoir writer faces chapters that feel impossible to write or themes that seem too complex to explore, so be prepared to face those challenges.

- Write easier chapters first, and return to the difficult material when you have more momentum.

- Permit yourself to write poorly during the first draft. Focus on getting the story down rather than crafting perfect prose.

- Join memoir writing groups or work with other writers who understand the unique challenge of a personal narrative.

Readers appreciate authenticity, insight, and professional execution. Your unique experience is invaluable when it illuminates a universal truth - a truth that helps others to understand their own lives better.

Start with your story, but always remember - you're not just writing about your life - you are writing about the human experience, using your own life as a powerful example.

For Traumatic Memories

- Write in the third person first and later convert to first person.

- Start with just the facts, adding emotion and reflection later.

- Write the scene after the trauma rather than the trauma itself.

- Use writing prompts like - "What I remember most clearly..." or "The thing nobody understood..."

For Family Conflicts

- Focus on specific incidents rather than character generalizations.

- Write multiple versions from different perspectives before finding the truth that encompasses the complexity.

- Start by considering how the conflict affected you rather than focusing on who was right or wrong.

- Consider what you learned rather than what others did wrong.

For Embarrassing or Shameful Experiences

- Remember that vulnerability creates a connection with readers.

- Write about the shame itself as much as the shameful event.

- Consider how sharing this story might help others.

- Start with - "Something I never told anyone..."

For Complex Relationships

- Create lists of specific memories rather than trying to summarize an entire relationship.

- Write about contradictions - "He was the kind of person who..." followed by opposing examples.

- Focus on pivotal moments that reveal character rather than daily interactions.

- Consider how the relationship changed you rather than trying to explain the other person's behavior.

When You Feel Stuck

- Change your writing location or time of day.

- Interview family members or friends about their memories of events.

- Look through old photos to trigger forgotten details.

- Write letters to people in your story that you never send.

- Skip the difficult chapters and write easier ones first.

- The goal is forward momentum, not perfect prose.

- Permit yourself to write badly through difficult material - you can always revise it later when you have more emotional distance.

Your Story Matters

Writing a memoir takes courage. It requires examining your life honestly, sharing your vulnerability publicly, and trusting that your experience has value for others.

In a world increasingly hungry for authentic connection and real wisdom, your story can become exactly the book someone desperately needs to read.

The difference between a memoir that changes lives and one that sits unread isn't the drama of your experiences - it's the skill with which you present those experiences.

Every successful memoir author started with the same blank page you are facing now. The reason those people succeeded is not because their lives were more interesting than yours; it's because they learned to craft their stories in a way that engaged their audience.

Your memoir begins with a single page, written with honesty and hope. The rest is just craft and persistence - all of which you can learn and apply.

Chapter Ten
How to Write a Children's Book

THE CHILDREN'S BOOK market represents one of the most rewarding yet challenging segments of publishing. With over $1.7 billion in annual sales in the US alone, children's books offer a tremendous opportunity for authors willing to master the unique craft of writing for young readers.

Unlike adult fiction, children's books require authors to think like their audience, while writing with the sophistication of an adult. This delicate balance separates successful children's authors from those whose manuscripts never get off the ground.

Understanding Your Young Audience

Before you write a single word, you must understand that children are not simply small adults. They think differently, process information differently, and have vastly different attention spans depending on their age.

Ages 0 to 3 - Board Books

- These readers respond to rhythm, repetition, and simple concepts.

- Limit your vocabulary to 50-100 words, with large, bold illustrations carrying the story.

Ages 4 to 8 - Picture Books

- Stories should be 500-1000 words, with room for 32 pages of illustrations.

- Children this age love humor, simple adventure, and characters who solve their own problems.

Ages 6 to 10 - Early Readers

- These books bridge picture books and chapter books.

- The sentences are longer but still simple, with more text than pictures.

Ages 8 to 12 - Middle Grade

- Full chapter books with 20,000 to 50,000 words.

- Themes become more complex, addressing friendship, family, and growing up, but without the romantic elements of young adult fiction.

The Golden Rule

- Never write down to children. They can sense condescension a mile away, and will reject it immediately.

The Four Pillars of Children's Book Success

1. A Compelling Hook

- Children's books must grab their attention within the first few sentences.

- Adults might grant you a page or two, but children will abandon a boring book in seconds.

- Your opening should pose a question, present a problem, or introduce something unexpected.

- Instead of - "Tommy was a little boy who lived in a house with his mom and dad."

- Try - "Tommy's pet dinosaur was getting too big for the bathtub."

2. Authentic Dialogue and Voice

- Children speak differently than adults, but you should avoid stereotypical "kid speak" that sounds forced.

- Listen to real children in your target age group. Note their vocabulary, their concerns, and how they express emotions.

- The narrative voice should always match your intended audience.

- A picture book might use a warm, storytelling voice, while a middle-grade novel might use the protagonist's own voice with age-appropriate vocabulary and concerns.

3. Visual Storytelling
   - Chapter books for older children will benefit from visual thinking.

   - Children are visual learners who create mental movies as they read.

   - Your text needs to paint a clear and vivid picture without overwhelming young readers with elaborate descriptions.

   - Show emotions through actions rather than telling. For example - "Sarah's bottom lip trembled" works better than, "Sarah felt sad."

4. Meaningful Themes
- The best children's books tackle real issues that matter to kids - making friends, dealing with fears, handling disappointment, or learning to be brave.

- But these themes must emerge naturally from the story, not feel like lessons forced onto the narrative.

The Children's Book Writing Process

Step 1: Choose Your Age Group First
- This decision determines everything else; word count, complexity, themes, and publishing approach. Don't write a story and then try to figure out who it's for. That's like trying to run backwards.

Step 2: Develop Your Concept
- Children's books need a clear, simple concept that can be explained in one sentence. "A family of mice help a child overcome her fear of the dark," or "A

girl learns to appreciate her uniqueness when she starts a new school."

- Test your concept with the "so what?" question. Why should a child care about this story? What will they gain from reading it?

Step 3: Create Relatable Characters

- Child protagonists should be slightly older than your target audience - four-year-olds want to read about five-year-olds for example.

- Your character needs a clear goal, obstacles to overcome, and the ability to solve their own problems.

- Avoid creating perfect children. Kids relate to characters who make mistakes, feel scared sometimes, or struggle with something. Give your protagonist both strengths and flaws.

Step 4: Structure Your Story

Children's books follow a simple three-act structure.

- **Setup:** Introduce character and problem.

- **Challenge:** Character attempts to solve problem, often failing at first.

- **Resolution:** Character succeeds through their own efforts and growth.

Keep the timeline short. A picture book might cover a single day, while a middle-grade novel rarely spans more than a school year.

Step 5: Write Your First Draft
- Don't over-think this stage. Get the story down, focusing on the essential elements of character, problem, and solution. You can refine the language and pacing in revision.

- For picture books, think in terms of page turns. Each spread should advance the story and end with something that makes the reader want to turn the page.

Common Mistakes That Spoil Children's Books

Mistake 1: Trying to Teach Instead of Entertain

- Children can smell a lesson coming from pages away. Focus on telling a great story; any lessons should emerge naturally.

Mistake 2: Adult Protagonists Solving Problems

- Children want to read about kids who handle their own challenges. Parents and teachers can provide support, but the child character must drive the solution.

Mistake 3: Inappropriate Length

- Each age group has specific word count expectations. A 2,000 word picture book will be rejected immediately, regardless of how good the story is.

Mistake 4: Outdated References
- Children live in the present. Avoid references that will date your book, or that modern children won't understand.

Mistake 5: Underestimating Your Audience
- Children are clever, intuitive, and have sophisticated emotional lives. They deserve stories that respect their intelligence.

The Business Side of Children's Publishing

Traditional Publishing
- Children's books released by traditional publishers are typically presented by an agent. The market is extremely competitive, with major publishers receiving thousands of submissions annually.

- If you decide to approach literary agents, research which ones represent your specific age category. A picture book agent might not represent middle-grade novels for example.

- Your query letter should be shorter than for adult fiction - no more than one page.

Self-Publishing Considerations

Self-publishing children's books presents unique challenges, particularly when it comes to the cost of professional illustrations for picture books. A quality illustrator can cost $3,000-$15,000 for a 32-page picture book.

However, self-publishing does offer several advantages:

- Complete creative control.

- Higher royalties.

- The ability to target niche markets that traditional publishers may ignore.

The Illustration Factor

- Unless you are a professional illustrator, don't include any artwork with your submission to traditional publishers or literary agents. Editors prefer to choose their own illustrators.

- If you decide to self-publish, invest in professional illustration. Children judge books by their covers and pictures more than any other audience.

- Second-rate illustrations will ruin even the best story.

Where to Begin?

Start with Your Strengths

- If you are a teacher, you will understand child development.

- If you are a parent, you know what resonates with kids.

- If you have a background in art, you might consider illustrating your own book.

- Start with what you already know and build on that.

Join the Community
- Organizations like the Society of Children's Book Writers and Illustrators (SCBWI) provide education, networking, and critique opportunities.

- Members of the children's book community are very welcoming to newcomers who approach them professionally.

- The SCBWI:

Test Your Work

Read your stories aloud to children in your target age group. Their reactions will tell you more than any adult critique. Do they stay engaged? Do they ask questions? Do they want to hear it again?

The Path Forward

Writing successful children's books requires an understanding of the storytelling craft, and the unique needs of young readers. It demands respect for your audience, patience with the revision process, and persistence in a competitive market.

The rewards, however, extend far beyond financial success. Children's book authors have the opportunity to shape young minds, introduce children to the joy of reading, and create stories that families will treasure for generations.

Your journey as a children's book author begins with a single story and a deep respect for the remarkable audience you are writing for. Children are the most honest readers you will ever encounter - and ultimately, the most rewarding to serve.

Remember, every child who falls in love with books because of your story becomes a lifelong reader.

And that alone is a legacy worth pursuing.

CHAPTER ELEVEN

Title and Subtitle

THE TITLE AND subtitle of your book are extremely important and need to be:

- Enticing to Potential Readers

- Relevant to your Genre

- Relevant to your Story

And above all,

- Search Engine Friendly - Amazon is a search engine just like Google.

When I say 'Search Engine Friendly,' that means your title or, more likely, your subtitle contain the sort of words that people who are looking to buy a book like yours will type into the search bar on Amazon.

- You must always include a subtitle when you publish your book. It may not appear on your book's cover, but it will make your book more visible and more discoverable on Amazon.

- Amazon pays just as much attention to a book's subtitle as its title when matching a book with the keywords people enter into the search bar.

We will discuss keywords and keyword research shortly. Still, you should understand that there is a hierarchy of emphasis and authority regarding search term keywords on Amazon.

- Amazon gives the most emphasis and authority to keywords that appear in a book's title or subtitle.

- It puts less, but considerable, emphasis on the keywords entered in the seven Keyword Boxes that appear on your book's Set-Up Page on Amazon KDP.

- It gives little (but still some) emphasis to keywords that appear in your Book Description and reviews.

Don't bother trying to stuff your Book Description with keywords. Just write the best one you can and present a compelling and engaging narrative that will resonate with your target reader and appeal to your audience.

You can use story elements for your book's title, as well as character names, times, and dates.

- Murder on the Orient Express

- Robinson Crusoe

- 1984

Keep your title short and simple, using your subtitle to explain more about the book, and capture people's attention when they are searching for books on Amazon.

If your book is a memoir about you learning Italian and your subsequent travels in Italy, then put those words in the subtitle of your book, including the word - memoir.

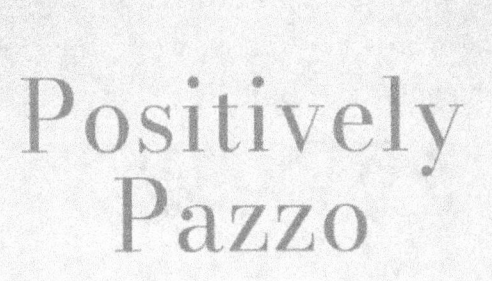

If you are a clumsy and optimistic New Yorker who has written a funny book about starting a gardening business in Connecticut, include words like funny, work, business and gardening in the subtitle.

Validate Your Book Idea

It is vital to know if there is a market for your book and that people are willing to pay for a book like yours.

- Having identified your audience and outlined your book, go to the Books page of Amazon and enter the keywords that someone might type into the search bar if they were looking for a book like yours, and see what Amazon's predictive text suggests.

- Once you find a relevant and worthwhile keyword phrase, click 'Search' and see how many results appear each time. More than twenty thousand results would suggest that is a very competitive keyword, and you may want to narrow your search term.

- Importantly, if the first three or four books that appear in any keyword search do not belong on the same shelf as your book in a bookstore, then that's not a viable keyword to include in your title or subtitle.

- For example, you may consider including the words, 'An Italian Escape' in your subtitle, because your book is a memoir about the run-down cottage you purchased in a remote Tuscan village. Still, when you enter that search term into Amazon, the first few books that show up are about a prison break during the Second World War, or the head of a mafia clan who continues to escape justice in Sicily.

- Research similar titles in your genre, see what other publishers are doing, and ask the opinion of librarians, bookstores, friends, and family.

- Also, search Amazon for your book title and author name (separately) and make sure they don't clash with an already famous book or author.

- You will probably clash with something or someone, and that's okay, but don't take on a book that is already very successful, and if your name is Stephen King, use a pen name.

- Using a pen name while managing and accessing an Amazon account under your own name is perfectly fine.

- You can even publish some books under your name and others with a pen name using the same account. That's what I do, and it works perfectly well.

Chapter Twelve
Editing your Book

SEEK HONEST, CONSTRUCTIVE, worthwhile feedback (before you publish) and give your manuscript to an independent third party (ideally an experienced editor or a creative writing tutor) to assess.

Don't give it to your family or your friends. That's a waste of time. They will just tell you it's great. You may tell them, "I want you to be completely honest." They will still tell you it's great.

All the same, carefully research and consider any editor that you may decide to work with.

Ensure they have experience with and a solid understanding of your book's subject.

Anyone can call themselves an editor. But there are editors, and there are editors.

I have used a website called Reedsy in the past.

- Reedsy:

Reedsy has a section called Marketplace that presents the details and credentials of several freelance editors.

I found my editor, Rosanna, on Reedsy. She did an outstanding job with my book Yards and Stripes, before she became a librarian and decided that she didn't have the time to do freelance editing any longer.

Since then, I have found one or two other so-called 'editors and proofreaders' who were (to say the least) less helpful and, frankly, more expensive.

Study an editor's credentials and reviews before contacting anyone, as editing can be costly, and finding the right person is essential.

A couple of AI programs are a viable alternative to working with an editor.

- Grammarly:

or

- Pro-Writing Aid:

- Both Grammarly and Pro Writing Aid have both free and paid versions. They will identify punctuation and spelling errors and suggest alterations to your text that you can either accept or dismiss.

- The free versions will only identify a few errors, and it is a good idea to subscribe to either program while you proofread your final manuscript.

- You can leave either program open on your computer, and it will identify errors and suggest alternatives as you write - anything from documents to emails. Personally, that drives me up the wall, so I open them when I choose to, copy and paste a chapter at a time, and work through that.

- Above all, you must get your book in the best possible shape it can be, to stand any chance of making it a commercial success, whether you intend to submit it to a traditional publisher or publish it yourself.

- If that means re-writing it, then re-writing it, and re-writing it again, then that's what you do.

- You can rest assured that countless successful authors have done exactly that many times before you.

- I know I have.

Proofreading

Once you have completed your manuscript, you need to proofread it meticulously.

Read it aloud and read it backward if need be.

I am one of the world's worst proofreaders, and I often fail to identify words I haven't even typed on the page.

One day, I told a woman in my Italian class how frustrating I found the whole proofreading process, when she said, "It doesn't have to be perfect," and I replied, "Well, that's just it. It does."

- You can get away with a few missing commas here and there, but never spelling mistakes and missing words.

- Traditionally published books will very occasionally contain mistakes, but rarely, and just as a second-rate cover will flag your book as 'third-rate self-published,' so too will apparent errors in spelling and punctuation.

- When you finalize your manuscript, you need to create a Word file document that has every element you want to include in your book.

- You need a page devoted to the book's title, subtitle, and author name, also a copyright notice, disclaimer, any dedication, a list of contents, chapter headings, and at the end of the book a Note from the Author asking people to write a review.

- This final document is what your publisher or book formatter will work with, and they can only work with what you give them.

- Always include a claim of Copyright, and if you are writing a non-fiction book add a Disclaimer.

- Use the Copyright claim and Disclaimer at the start of this book as templates.

Chapter Thirteen

Traditional or Self-Publishing?

IF YOUR PAPERBACK sells for $14.99, you may receive a royalty of $1.20 (most likely less) per sale from a traditional publisher.

However, you can publish that same book yourself, sell it for the same price, and earn $4.00 to $5.00 per sale, but you must invest time, money, and effort in so doing.

When you publish your book, you set your own prices, and you can secure a much greater return (per sale) than you would with a traditional publisher.

The distribution of your book can be just as broad, the only difference is that bookstores are unlikely to stock it, and they will need to order your book in when someone asks for it.

And just because your book is traditionally published, don't assume it will be available in bookstores. Millions of books are on the market, and any bookstore will, at best, only stock a few thousand titles.

I was able to eavesdrop on a conversation in a local bookstore one day when a sales rep from a major publisher called into the store to speak with the owner.

I had been speaking with the owner just minutes before, and she invited me to listen in, so I stood close by, acting like a customer browsing through a few titles on the shelves.

The sales rep called in with the publisher's latest New Releases Catalog.

Their conversation lasted less than a minute.

The store owner asked, "So which ones do I want?" and the sales rep presented her with a colorful catalog of book covers, saying, "You want that one," before he flicked over a couple of pages and said, "That one." After flicking past several more pages, he added, "And that one."

The store owner said, "I don't want any of these others?" and the sales rep said, "Nope."

She ordered five copies of each of the three books he had 'suggested.'

Later, I asked her, "How many books did that catalog feature?"

"Maybe a hundred," she said.

- Traditional publishers sell eBooks for grossly inflated prices - sometimes as much as $12.99, from which you, as an author, may earn about $2.50.

- This pricing structure is in place because traditional publishers must protect and maintain their relationships with bookstores. The cost of producing an eBook copy of your book to a publisher is negligible. Still, they can't afford to undermine their distribution network by selling eBooks for significantly less than print books. If they did, bookstores would go out of business, the entire publishing model would collapse, and everyone would be self-publishing.

- You, on the other hand, can sell your eBook for $4.99 and make $3.50 - 70%, a significantly better royalty than you will secure with a traditional publisher, while selling your eBook for less than half the price.

- Traditional publishers almost certainly don't sell as many eBooks as they do print books. They do make a significant margin on those sales, however.

- You don't as an author, but publishers do.

Of course, if you publish your book, you have to cover all the costs yourself with no guarantee that you will ever sell a single copy and earn anything at all.

Sadly, this is true for many books and authors. However, there are several things you can do to give yourself the best possible chance of making your book a commercial success. And implementing all of the advice outlined in this book would be a good start.

We will cover all of the costs involved in greater detail shortly.

As a guide, I suggest you allow $4,000 in your first twelve months, which means you will need to sell about 1,000 books to break even.

All the same, I suggest you set your goals over a much longer timeframe than one year.

- Importantly, readers don't care who publishes your book. If they think they will like it, they may well buy it. They are not going to investigate who the publisher is before they do. Still, your book must be presented just as professionally as any traditionally published title.

- Book buyers perceive self-published books as 'third rate,' simply because so many people continue to publish books with second-rate covers, sloppy formatting, and spelling mistakes. And these books are indeed third-rate.

- The fact is, Amazon doesn't care if people publish third-rate books on its platform. It costs them nothing to offer those books for sale, and they are happy for their customers to decide whether or not they are any good.

Chapter Fourteen
Formatting

ONCE YOUR MANUSCRIPT is complete, and if you decide to self-publish, you need to format it as an eBook and a paperback. You can have a hardcover version formatted as well, but I suggest you focus on an eBook and paperback initially.

- eBook dimensions are standard, while paperback and hardcover dimensions vary. There are industry standard sizes, however.

- I suggest 5.5 x 8.5 inches for a paperback of 60,000 words or more and 5 x 8 inches for 50,000 words.

- Check these dimensions with a book formatter and your cover designer.

- Formatting involves typesetting the text, contents, chapter headings, paragraph indentations, page numbers, photographs, and illustrations.

- In short, everything that appears from inside the front cover to inside the back.

- Every element in your manuscript needs to appear in the same sequence and in the same manner that you want it to appear in your book. If you want Chapter Ten to appear with Ten as a word, then be sure to type Chapter Ten, not Chapter 10. The same goes for upper and lower case or all capitals.

- Book formatters will only faithfully reproduce what you give them. They can't read your mind.

These days, I work with a specialist book formatter who is an author herself. Her name is Alice, and she lives in, of all places, Romania.

She is the third book formatter I have worked with to date and the only one I will ever work with again. She does a brilliant job, and you can find her on Fiverr.

- Fiverr - Alice Iza:

- There are a handful of book formatting software programs available, and if this is a task you want to tackle yourself, then the best of these is undoubtedly a program called Atticus.

- Atticus has been developed by the people at Kindlepreneur, and in the short time it has been available, it has generated some excellent reviews.

- Atticus Book Formatting:

Above all, it is imperative that the formatting of your book is as neat and professional as any book published by any traditional publisher.

- Once this process is complete, you or your book formatter will create an ePub file (a universal eBook format) and a PDF for your paperback version.

- A book formatter may also send you a formatted file in Microsoft Word. This way, if you need to make any minor changes or corrections, you can amend the Word file yourself and re-save it as a PDF without incurring any extra costs.

- If you need to amend an ePub file, you can download a free eBook editing program called Calibre.

- Calibre eBook Editing:

- Upload your original ePub file to Calibre, then right-click on the file name, choose Edit, make the necessary changes, and re-save it.

- Your PDF file will give you a page count for your paperback, which your cover designer will use to calculate the spine width of your book, so be sure to make a careful note of it.

- Next you need to secure an ISBN (International Standard Book Number) for your paperback and also for your eBook.

- You can get away without buying an ISBN for your eBook, but many eBook distributors will require one and not having an ISBN for your eBook will limit the reach of your distribution.

- Amazon will give your eBook an ISBN for free but only if you make your eBook exclusive to Amazon.

- I suggest that you secure an ISBN for each version of your book; one for the eBook, one for the paperback, one for your audiobook, and one for a hardback version.

- You can secure individual ISBNs or a batch of ten from a company called Bowker.

- Bowker ISBNs:

- An ISBN is a unique thirteen-digit numerical code that identifies your book, and this is what your cover designer will use to create a barcode that will appear on the back cover of your paperback.

- Your next step is to commission your cover design - applying the three Golden Rules. You should also consider having an audiobook cover designed and an animated cover (created by Damonza) that you can use as a marketing tool in the future.

- Once your manuscript has been formatted (as both an eBook and a paperback) and you have a cover design that you are thrilled with, it's almost time to publish your book.

- Be sure to let your cover designer know that your paperback or hardcover book will feature a barcode. That way, they can allow space for it on the back cover.

Getting Reviews

Getting reviews for your book is always helpful, as reviews don't just demonstrate social proof, they help to improve your book's Sales Rank on Amazon. And the best way to get a review is to ask for one.

At the end of your book, include - A Note from the Author, thanking people for reading it and asking (if they enjoyed it) to leave a short review on the website where they bought it.

Many people may feel reluctant to write a review, so assure them that, "Just a few words would really help."

Hardcovers

Formatting a hardcover version of your book is a separate exercise, as is its cover design.

A hardcover version is something to consider once your book is selling well as a paperback and/or an eBook. So, too, is producing an audiobook.

We will discuss audiobooks in more detail in Chapter 22.

Chapter Fifteen

Keywords and Categories

TWO ESSENTIAL ELEMENTS to consider when setting your book up on Amazon (and with other platforms) are Keywords and Categories.

Categories

Think of categories as the area of a bookstore where people can find your book.

- History

- Self-Help

- Murder Mystery

- Travel

- Health and Well-Being

- Language Learning

- Your book must be allocated to its most relevant and appropriate categories, as people search for books on Amazon by category and also by keyword search term.

- With Amazon, you can allocate your book to three categories, so you need to find three categories that are relevant to your book and not hugely competitive.

- It is better to rank well in a less competitive category than be way off the pace in a very popular one.

- Always remember that Amazon rewards relevance. Never place your book in an obscure, irrelevant category to try and game the system. That simply won't work.

Keywords

Amazon KDP displays seven Keyword Boxes on your book's Set-Up Page, where you can enter as many as fifty characters in each box.

The keywords you need to enter in these boxes are the sort of words that, in isolation or combination, people are likely to enter into the search bar when they are looking for a book like yours on Amazon.

For example, if you were to include the keywords:

- murder mystery thriller small town

Amazon will index your book for search terms such as:

- murder

- thriller

- mystery

- murder mystery

- mystery thriller

- small town murder mystery

and so on.

- The idea is to enter single keywords that people are likely to search for and search terms that may feature those same words in combination.

- People searching for books on Amazon will often start with a generic search term such as - murder mystery and then narrow subsequent searches to eventually end up with - murder mystery set in a small town.

- Don't waste any of your fifty characters (this includes spaces) with words such as - a, an, in, of, by, or any plurals, as the algorithm will pick those up anyway. The same principle applies to words like book, ebook, kindle, and audiobook.

- One method of identifying viable keywords is to simply enter those words into the search bar on Amazon and see what its predictive text suggests.

- You can enter a word like - mystery followed by the letters a, b, then c, d, e, and so on, and see what words and phrases Amazon suggests.

A much better way to enact this process is to invest in a software program called Publisher Rocket.

Publisher Rocket is a concept developed and marketed by Dave Chesson and his team at Kindlepreneur.

- The Publisher Rocket program harvests and presents Amazon search data for specific search term keywords, phrases, and categories.
- The software presents separate search data and category selections from Amazon stores in the USA, UK,

Canada, Australia, Germany, France, Italy and Spain.

- Enter a particular keyword or phrase into the Keyword Search feature, and Publisher Rocket will present you with the number of searches that particular keyword generates per month in any of those individual countries.

- The viability of individual keyword search terms is identified by a simple number system, together with an associated color - green, amber, or red, depending upon how competitive the program believes any particular keyword is and how difficult it will be for your book to rank for it

- The higher the score, the more difficult that keyword will be to rank for.

- The program highlights competitive keyword scores in red, less competitive ones in amber, and more viable ones in green.

- The same color scheme applies to a keyword's overall Competition Score, which the program calculates using factors such as the number of searches, average monthly sales generated from those searches, and the overall competition for that particular keyword phrase.

- What's more, Publisher Rocket's color system will identify keywords that may generate a lot of searches, but result in very few sales.

- Publisher Rocket is also an excellent tool when it comes to selecting the three categories that you will allocate your book to on Amazon. It will even highlight what it calls Ghost Categories, which are categories that Amazon may allocate your book to but that shoppers cannot find while searching for books by category. Never allocate your book to a Ghost Category.

- The Reverse ASIN Lookup feature allows you to enter the details of a competitor's book and see what keywords Amazon has indexed for that particular title.

- The Reverse ASIN feature is a brilliant addition to the program. It's like spying on your competition, but in an entirely legitimate and perfectly legal way.

- There is a great deal more to the program than I have outlined here, and it is constantly updated (free of charge) to those who invested a couple of hundred dollars to buy it in the first place.

- Publisher Rocket is a program that major publishers have been using for several years, and it is an essential tool for any self-published author.

- You can use Publisher Rocket to measure the commercial viability of your book before you publish it, confirm your book's title and subtitle, and thereafter increase your book's visibility and discoverability to buyers on Amazon with a selection of carefully researched keywords.

- You can even identify which major publishers are publishing books that are allocated to your particular genre or category.

- Publisher Rocket is the best investment you will ever make as a self-published author.

- Publisher Rocket:

Chapter Sixteen
Keyword Strategy

WHEN CHOOSING AND entering keywords onto your book's KDP Set-Up Page the most important things to remember are relevance and structure.

The team at Kindlepreneur recently conducted a fascinating research study on how authors and publishers should best structure and enter their book's keywords on Amazon KDP.

The recommendations from which are as follows;

- Devote your first three keyword boxes (vertically on the left-hand side) to three specific search term phrases that people are likely to enter in the Amazon search bar when looking for a book like yours.

- Usually, you wouldn't repeat the same word in more than one keyword box. However, in this instance, we are looking for an exact match with one of these three specific keyword phrases, so repeating a word is okay.

For example:

- witty travel memoir Italy

- Italy language vacation

- learning Italian vacation

Publisher Rocket is a tremendous asset because rather than simply entering keywords into the search bar on Amazon and seeing what pops up, you can enter those same keywords into the program and see how many searches they generate each month, together with an indication of how competitive each keyword search term is.

- As a rule of thumb, I suggest you find at least one specific keyword search term that generates more than 100 searches a month and that has a competition score of less than 20 on Publisher Rocket.

- The more monthly searches your keyword phrase generates, the better. Still, I suggest you don't enter a number one specific keyword phrase that has a competition score of more than 20 - at least not to begin with.

- The idea is for your book to rank on the first page of search results for your three specific keyword phrases on Amazon. The higher each keyword's competition score, the less likely that is to happen, and you are much better off with your book listed on page one for a keyword phrase that generates 200 searches a month than on page three or four for a keyword phrase that generates 2,000 searches a month.

- **Top Tip:** 96% of people searching for books on Amazon never get beyond the first page of search results. Rather than continue onto page two or three (if they can't find what they are looking for), they will refine their search term and start over.

- Your goal is to generate a regular pattern of sales, however modest that may be initially, from your specific keywords in particular, as these sales will continue to improve the rankings for all of your other keywords.

- If your book can achieve a regular pattern of sales - one or two copies a day for a couple of weeks may suffice; then Amazon will reward your book by elevating its Sales Rank, improving your overall rankings, and showing your book to more people.

- Find at least one relevant, specific keyword phrase that generates more than a hundred searches a month, with the lowest competition score possible. A score of less than ten would be great.

- The idea is that your book ranks number one on Amazon for an exact match of that keyword phrase.

- If your book ranks number one for a search term that generates perhaps two hundred searches a month, that may be enough to sell at least one copy every two or three days, which may, in turn, be enough to improve the ranking of several other search terms (comprising your other keywords), so they also appear on the first page of search results.

- The following two boxes (bottom left and top right of the two columns) should be devoted to General Keywords.

- In this instance, enter keywords relevant to your book, that people enter into the Amazon search bar individually or in combination.

- Finally, devote the last two boxes (bottom right) to keywords related to the three categories you have allocated your book to on Amazon.

- This last element is easy to do with the help of Publisher Rocket. Find the Kindle and Print categories you plan to allocate your book to, click on the Keywords tab on the right-hand side, and you will see a list of relevant keywords for that category.

- Using at least some keywords related to your book's category is essential. Otherwise, Amazon may decide to allocate your book to a different category altogether.

- Don't repeat any words in your general or category keywords, and don't enter your book's title, subtitle, or author name, as they are already indexed.

- Above all, never enter another book's title or author's name as a keyword. Entering keywords of this nature violates Amazon's Terms of Service, and doing so may lead to your account being suspended.

In summary, ensure that all the keywords you enter into the seven Keyword Boxes on your KDP Set-Up page are relevant to your book, and never include any words that are not.

When I first implemented this keyword strategy for my book - Positively Pazzo my rankings and sales improved almost overnight.

I had researched the keyword search term data relevant to my book on Publisher Rocket, and everything was tracking beautifully.

Then I got greedy.

I had seen search term keywords such as - Italian for Beginners and Learn Italian for Beginners generate thousands of searches every month.

My book is a light-hearted and amusing memoir of me learning Italian and traveling to Italy. It is not a textbook for people learning Italian.

Still, I thought, "Everything is going so well. Why not swap out one of these 'lesser keywords' and include the word 'beginner' instead?"

"After all, it's only one word. What could possibly go wrong?"

The next day, my rankings fell off a cliff.

Search terms that my book had ranked #1 for now ranked #10, and those I had ranked #7 for now ranked in the twenties and thirties.

By including the word 'beginner,' I had confused the Amazon algorithm as to exactly what my book was.

The algorithm couldn't be sure if my book was an amusing language learning/travel memoir or a textbook for people wanting to learn the Italian language.

Once I realized what had happened, I reinstated my original keywords, deleting the word 'beginner.'

A few days later, Amazon had largely restored my rankings.

- Three things really matter when it comes to keywords on Amazon.

Relevance, Relevance and Relevance.

- It is very easy to be seduced by the Sirens' Song of strong monthly search data, but never let that be at the expense of relevance.

Top Tip: You can amend and update your Book Description and keywords on Amazon, Ingram Spark, and Draft2Digital as often and whenever you like, but never change too many things at any one time on Amazon.

Each time you change your keywords, Amazon will recalibrate your book's metadata, and your rankings may suffer in the short term, while it does.

I once changed the order of three individual words in three different Keyword Boxes simultaneously, thinking it was "just one word in each of three different Keyword Boxes." The words themselves remained the same, and only the order was different.

"Surely that won't matter?" I thought.

My rankings plunged almost immediately and took several days to recover.

- If need be, change a word or two in just one Keyword Box, then wait another two or three days before changing anything in another Keyword Box, and so on.

- Amazon's algorithms are very complicated, and it is impossible to know which keywords work in conjunction with and help to underpin others.

- Once your book is ranking well, by all means, make a few changes, but execute the process gradually.

Top Tip #2: You will enter keywords for your eBook and keywords for your paperback separately on your book Set-Up Pages on Amazon KDP, and even though you can research Kindle and Print keywords separately on Publisher Rocket, Amazon suggests that you enter the same keywords, with the same structure for both versions of your book - eBook and paperback

Amazon doesn't explain exactly why. Still, if they say it's a good idea to do this, that's good enough for me.

Chapter Seventeen
Uploading Your Book to Amazon

WHEN YOU ARE ready to publish your book, you need to upload both your ePub eBook file and your PDF paperback file to Amazon Kindle Direct Publishing.

- Amazon Kindle Direct Publishing:

You will also upload your PDF paperback file to Ingram Spark and once your initial 90-day eBook exclusivity period with Amazon KDP Select (outlined in Chapter Seventeen) is completed, you will also upload your ePub file to Draft2Digital.

- Sign in to Amazon KDP with an existing Amazon account. If you don't already have an account, you will need to create one.

- Next, Amazon will present you with a User Agreement that you must read, understand, and agree to.

- You will then see your Author Dashboard.

- Make sure to complete all the personal information that Amazon asks you to enter before moving on - particularly your bank account details and tax status.

- Now click the large yellow button that reads - Create, and select - Create eBook on the next screen.

- This will open your eBook Set-Up Page.

- First, select the language in which you wrote your book, followed by your book's title and subtitle.

- Be sure to enter the correct capitalization of your title and subtitle.

  Title: Positively Pazzo

  Subtitle: Learning Italian and Travels in Italy. A Memoir.

  Not;

  Title: Positively pazzo

  Subtitle: Learning Italian and travels in Italy. A memoir

- The elements below your title and subtitle (Series and Number) are only relevant if your eBook is one of a series of books, so leave these two parts blank.

- Next, enter your author or pen name and the names of any other contributors you want to recognize - an illustrator or photographer, for example.

- Now paste in the Book Description that you formatted in HTML code with the Kindlepreneur Book Description Generator.

- Kindlepreneur Book Description Generator:

- Publishing Rights is where you confirm that you are the original creator of your content, own the copyright, and hold the publishing rights to your book.

- Now confirm your primary Amazon marketplace (which is where you expect to sell the most books), whether or not your book has any explicit content, and a recommended age range. This is more relevant for children's books, otherwise a minimum age of 18 + is a safe option.

- Categories and keywords are very important, so do your research with Publisher Rocket before completing this section, and follow the keyword structure detailed in the previous chapter.

- You can make your eBook available for pre-order at the base of the page. Pre-orders allow people to order a copy of your book before it is even published, which may be viable if you have a large and established social media following. Of course, in this instance, you are already uploading and publishing your book, so you don't need to bother with this.

- Now, click Save and Continue, and you will arrive on your eBook's Content Page.

- Your first option is whether or not to enable Digital Rights Management.

- Digital Rights Management is designed to stop unauthorized copying or distribution of your content. This sounds like a good idea, but selecting DRM will restrict people's ability to read your eBook on various devices (other than a Kindle) and prohibit them from sharing it with their friends. I suggest you don't tick this box.

- Next, you will upload the ePub file that your book formatter prepared for you or that you created yourself with Atticus.

- Now, upload the JPG eBook cover that an experienced, professional, specialist book cover designer created for you, and ignore the Cover Creator option entirely.

- The Kindle eBook Previewer lets you see how your eBook will appear on a Kindle device or the Kindle Reading App. The Previewer is an essential final check to ensure that your eBook is formatted correctly and there are no apparent errors.

- Finally, add your ISBN at the base of the page, then click Save and Continue.

- Enroll in KDP Select for 90 days when you first publish your eBook so that you can schedule five days of free eBook giveaways. Refer to Chapter Seventeen for details.

- Select all territories and a 70% royalty unless you intend to sell your eBook at a significant discount, in which case you may be obliged to select a 35% royalty option.

- Next, you must select individual eBook prices in all Amazon marketplaces.

- Pricing will require a degree of research, which you can do by searching for similar eBooks on Amazon and also with Publisher Rocket, which can tell you what price other eBooks are selling for.

- I usually start by pricing my eBooks at US $4.99 and calculate other countries' pricing based on the US price before adjusting them to a .99 cent price point.

- I suggest you don't follow the lead of traditional publishers, who often price their eBooks at $12.99 or more. You can still make a good margin on an eBook priced at $4.99, and it is better to sell two or three books at this price than none at $12.99.

- You can discount your eBook and sell it for as little as 99 cents. Still, I would be wary of creating a perception that your eBook is only worth that much.

- You may see a notice at the base of this last page alerting you that some of your Account Information is incomplete. If so, return to the relevant section and fill in any missing detail.

- Otherwise, click Save, and your eBook is uploaded.

The process for uploading your paperback is essentially the same. You just need to upload your PDF paperback file and a PDF of your paperback cover.

Once you have uploaded your eBook, you should have no trouble repeating the process with your paperback.

When you upload your paperback, be sure NOT to select the box that is marked Amazon Expanded Distribution. Let Ingram

Spark distribute your paperback to other online retailers, bookstores and libraries. Bookstores are not overly fond of the world's biggest online book retailer, and many will refuse to order or stock a book that is exclusively distributed by Amazon.

Be aware that it can take up to 72 hours before your books are approved and become available.

In any case, Amazon will send you an email confirming the publication of each format of your book or you can check on your Author Dashboard.

Chapter Eighteen

Other Elements

Amazon A+ Content

AN ELEMENT THAT will enhance your book's Detail Page is Amazon A+ Content, which allows you to present colorful banners that appear below your Book Description.

These banners can include photographs and text featuring extracts from your book or customer reviews.

A+ Content helps your book's overall presentation appear more professional, and it's certainly worth investing the time and effort to create it.

Click on Create A+ Content for each version of your book on your Author Dashboard (listed under Promote and Advertise) and follow the prompts.

There are several options for sizes and shapes, and when it comes to uploading these banners, there are some helpful videos on Amazon KDP to study.

Author Central

Amazon Author Central is a page where you can post your Author Profile, together with a photograph, and list all of the books you have published on Amazon KDP, together with any Editorial Reviews you may want to feature on your book Detail Pages.

- Author Central helps readers learn more about you and perhaps discover other books you may have published. It also helps to establish your credibility as an author.

- You can also incorporate the address of your author profile in your email signature. That way anyone you communicate with can discover your books.

- Don't underestimate the value of a well presented Author Bio. Particularly for a nonfiction book. A strong bio builds trust. It positions you as someone worth listening to, and it gives readers one more reason to buy your book. If you have a lot of experience or any awards, relating to the content of your book, include that in your Author Bio.

Look Inside Feature

When you set your books up on Amazon KDP, be sure to enable its Look Inside Feature.

This feature replicates the process of someone taking your book off the shelf in a bookstore and reading the first sentence, paragraph, or the first few pages.

The first sentence of your book sets the tone for what follows, and readers will grant you more time and attention if your first sentence engages them immediately.

- **Positively Pazzo** - If my friend Emily had a credit card, I may have never written this book.

- **Yards and Stripes** - It was conceived as a grand adventure.

It doesn't have to be earth-shattering but it does need to be interesting and engaging.

- Books sell by word of mouth, and your job is to kick-start that process. Firstly by writing a great book with a great title, an outstanding cover, and a first-rate Book Description, and then by getting it in front of the right people, who will buy it, read it, and tell others about it.

- This task is not easy. The whole process is very challenging. It's like riding a bicycle up a steep hill. It is hard work, and your leg muscles are screaming, but when you get over the top of that hill and roll down the other side quite effortlessly (making money in your sleep), it's the best feeling in the world.

- Regardless of whether your book is traditionally or self-published, whenever anyone asks you, "Where can I buy your book?" always tell them to buy it on Amazon.

- If you are self-published, you will earn a better royalty with Amazon than you will from any other retailer.

- More importantly, every sale you make on Amazon helps your Sales Rank, and the better your Sales Rank, the more visible and discoverable your book will become.

- And you don't have to sell hundreds of books every day for that to happen. Amazon's algorithms will recognize and reward books with a consistent sales record, more so than books that might secure a short-term spike in sales, for example. If you can consistently sell one or two books a day for perhaps a couple of weeks, that may be enough to see your book climb the rankings and become more discoverable to people searching for books on Amazon.

- It's as if all the algorithms get together on a Monday morning to discuss how books are selling, before one of them mentions your book, telling the others that it is selling consistently, even though it doesn't yet have a very good Sales Rank.

- Before you know it, the other algorithms agree; they all get on board, and your book gets more exposure before climbing the charts.

- Whether people are searching by keyword or category, it is essential that your book features on the first page of search results, ideally #1.

- Statistically, 27% of people conducting a generic search on Amazon will click on the book ranked #1, 12% on #2, and so on, while only 5 or 6% will click on the last couple of listings on the first page of search results with just 4% clicking on anything at all listed on page two.

Of course, your book will have an outstanding cover, and you will almost certainly do better than this.

Chapter Nineteen

Distribution and Royalties

THE DISTRIBUTION STRATEGY that I suggest you adopt is as follows:

- Amazon Kindle Direct Publishing - eBook and paperback.

- Ingram Spark - paperback to bookstores, libraries, and other online retailers.

- Draft2Digital - eBook to online retailers other than Amazon.

- Findaway Voices - Distributes audiobooks to Audible, Storytel, and several other online retailers.

- Publishing your eBook and paperback on Amazon will see your books available in all Amazon stores worldwide, and (after researching your competition) you will set your own prices in each territory.

- Let Ingram Spark distribute your paperback (worldwide) to other online retailers, bookstores, and libraries.

- Draft2Digital will distribute your eBook to online retailers, including Apple, Google, Barnes and Noble and any number of others.

- You will also set prices for your eBook in each territory (worldwide) with Draft2Digital.

- When you do, make sure your books are at least the same price as they are on Amazon in any particular marketplace. More expensive (with other retailers) is fine, but never make them cheaper. If you do Amazon will reduce the price of your book to match those prices anyway.

- You can upload your eBook to other online retailers yourself and secure a slightly better royalty than you will by distributing it with Draft2Digital. However, this is often a complicated exercise and, in my opinion, not worth the hassle.

Tax Status

Before you set up a publisher account with Amazon, Ingram Spark, or Draft2Digital, you will need to confirm your tax information or secure a non-resident tax status if you live outside the USA, which, in my case (several years ago) necessitated me calling the Office of Inland Revenue (on the phone) and taking part in an interview, which happily was a lot less painful than I had feared.

The process has changed since, and I suggest you follow the instructions on the Amazon Kindle Direct Publishing website.

- If you live outside the USA, you must secure a non-resident tax status; otherwise, things like a 30% Withholding Tax will significantly reduce your income.

- You will need to upload your tax information to each platform that you publish with.

- More often than not, your various distribution platforms will pay your royalty income in your local currency and transfer it to a local bank account in your country. Therefore, if you live outside the USA, you must enter your bank account details and a Swift Code. A Swift Code is an international identification code for your bank. You can search the Internet for your bank's

Swift Code or call them and ask what it is.

- Utilizing the distribution strategy I have outlined in this book (if you do decide to self-publish) will ensure your book is widely available all over the world and that your paperback is available for people to buy on a print-on-demand basis from bookstores and pretty much every major online retailer.

- If someone buys your book from Amazon, then Amazon prints your book, delivers your book to the customer, and pays you a royalty from that sale. You do not need to have a stock of paperbacks sitting in a box at home and be rushing to the post office each time you make a sale.

- Similarly, if someone buys your book from any other online retailer, then Ingram Spark prints your book and ships your book to the customer before paying you a royalty.

- The same process applies if someone buys or orders your book from a bookstore or borrows it from a library. Ingram Spark will print a copy of your book and deliver it to the relevant store or library.

- When you upload your book to Ingram Spark and set a pricing schedule/retailer discount (I suggest 50%), make sure you specify 'No Returns,' otherwise, bookstores (or anyone for that matter) can order a quantity of your book and return them to you if they don't sell. In this instance, you won't just be charged for the cost of printing the books but the cost of returning them to you.

- eBooks and audiobooks are downloaded more or less immediately. Those downloaded from KDP Select (if you choose to enroll) or other subscription-based libraries, may only generate a very modest royalty, but always remember that a sale is a sale, and you never know what may result from it. If someone is reading or listening to your book, that's a good thing.

- Something worth noting is that neither Amazon nor Ingram Spark will report a paperback sale (on their respective Author Dashboards) until the book is printed and shipped. So don't be concerned if someone tells you they bought a copy of your book and you can't see any record of it. Allow five to seven days for a paperback and eBooks one or two days.

- The Amazon KDP Dashboard, in particular, is very detailed. It will display sales of your eBooks and paperbacks separately, list all your free downloads, and present a breakdown of your royalties by book format and marketplace. You can also download reports of any previous month's earnings and payments.

- Sale reports from Ingram Spark and Draft2Digital are not as comprehensive although (just like Amazon) both companies will send you an email confirming each royalty payment.

- Royalties will be transferred to your designated bank account 60 days following the end of the month that Amazon (or other retailers) secured a sale. Therefore, you can expect to be paid anywhere from 60 to 90 days for sales of your book.

- Once you have published your paperback, you can order Author Copies for your own marketing, distribution or to sell yourself.

- I suggest you buy your Author Copies from Amazon, as in my experience, the quality of the paper and cover stock is better.

- These Author Copies will be delivered and billed to you at cost, plus postage.

Chapter Twenty
Book Launch

BELOW IS A Book Launch Budget (for your first year) listing all the elements that will help you to write, publish, and market your book.

Employing an editor is an optional extra, and even if you do hire an editor, I suggest you use a program like Grammarly as a spelling and punctuation checker to iron out any issues with your manuscript. Doing so will make an editor's job easier and save you money.

I have allowed an initial spend of $1,200 with Amazon Advertising ($100 per month) and an annual subscription to Publishing Performance of $360. I will introduce you to Publishing Performance in the next chapter.

You may invest less initially while the Publishing Performance AI program comes to grips with your book and audience. By the same token, I am confident you will have reason to invest more before long.

BOOK LAUNCH BUDGET

Publisher Rocket	$200
Grammarly - One month	$30
Formatting/Atticus	$150
ISBNs x ten - Bowker	$295
Cover Design - Damonza	$795
Launch Promotion	$300
Print Books x 10	$100
Publishing Performance (see Chapter 21)	$360
Amazon Ads	$1,200
Total	**$3,430**
Editor	$2,000
Total	**$5,430**

Launch Promotion

When you launch your book, it will not have any sales record, presence, reviews, or ranking on Amazon.

The idea then is to get as many people reading it as possible and as many (hopefully positive) reviews as possible.

- To do this, you will enact a Launch Promotion, whereby you give your eBook away free for five days.

- You will need to make your eBook (only your eBook) exclusive to Amazon for 90 Days. That means you won't be able to publish it with Draft2Digital for its first three months.

- When you upload your eBook to Amazon, make sure that you enroll in KDP Select. Enrolling in KDP Select will also allow people who subscribe to the Kindle Owners' Lending Library to download your eBook for free during that same 90-day period - from which you will receive a very modest royalty for each download. More importantly however, you can make your book free to download for any five days during those 90 days.

- You can also offer a reduced-price Countdown Deal, but I wouldn't bother with that when you first launch.

- Set your book's price to $4.99 when you first publish, before you make it free. This way people can see the 'normal price' is $4.99, which creates a perception of value.

- You then need to select three consecutive days soon after you publish, to make your eBook free, and another two consecutive days just before your 90-day period ends when you will also make it free to download.

- You will then pay various eBook promotion sites to email the details of your eBook (its cover and a short description) to all of their subscribers, giving them the details of when your eBook will be free to download on Amazon.

- Three days to start, two days to finish, and in between, price your eBook at $4.99 before you make it free again for two days, perhaps a week before your 90-day KDP Select period ends.

- I suggest you spend at least $200 on your first promotion and $100 on your second with as many different sites as possible.

- The dates you select on Amazon for your free eBook promotion will run from midnight USA Pacific Time, and while all this is going on, leave your paperback version priced normally in each Amazon marketplace.

- Below is a link to a list of eBook promotion websites, some of which are free. In contrast, others have a paid option, the cost of which will vary depending on the genre of your book and the corresponding size of their mailing lists.

- List of Free and Paid eBook Promotion Sites:

- It is worth including some of the free eBook promotion sites in addition to those that offer a paid option.

- The sites that are free will create an Amazon affiliate link for your book, which means they will receive a commission if anyone (having clicked on your free eBook link) buys anything else from Amazon in the 24 hours that follow. That's how and why they can offer their service for free.

- Some of the websites in this list have specific categories - Memoir, Romance, Crime, etc. with differing prices depending on the number of each category's subscribers.

- I suggest you focus on the Top Ten Paid Promotion sites listed in the article, and a different website (from the same list) to repeat the process after almost three months.

- When you set your paperback prices, Amazon will calculate and display your book's print cost and royalty.

- I suggest you aim to secure a paperback royalty of about $5.00 in the USA and perhaps £3.00 in the UK.

- Above all, study your competitors and price your book about the same as they do, or slightly less. Not significantly less, as that creates a perception that your book is 'second rate' and not as good.

- You can amend your prices at any time, but all the same, take your time doing this initially. Amazon will re-calculate your royalty each time you do, and there is no need to rush the process.

- And always use a price point of .99 cents. Retailers use this strategy for a reason. It works.

- Changes to any element of your book's metadata (which is everything from its content, its cover, keywords, description, or pricing will be updated quite quickly on Amazon, but it may take a few weeks to feed through to other retailers via Ingram Spark, and uploading a revised manuscript or a new cover to Ingram Spark (after more than 60 days) will attract a modest fee.

- The idea behind free eBook promotions is to present the opportunity to as many people as possible, to generate thousands of downloads and several reviews. If you can generate twenty reviews in the first instance and ten in the second, you have done well, and to be fair, reviews may take time to feed through, so don't be discouraged if they don't tumble in right away.

- The benefit of reviews is they demonstrate social proof, and the more reviews your book has, the more credible it appears.

- Tell your friends and family to download your eBook for free and ask them to write a review. Be aware, however, that to write a review, someone needs an Amazon account, and they need to have spent at least $50.00 on Amazon in the preceding twelve months.

And sadly, just because someone has downloaded your book for free, that doesn't mean they will write a positive review.

A woman from Mississippi downloaded a copy of my book *Yards and Stripes* for free as part of a launch promotion.

She then wrote a review that was titled - "A Piece of Irrelevant Trash."

That really hurt, and given her tirade sat at the top of my reviews for several months, it did me no favors at all.

If someone does write a review like that, whatever you do, don't hunt them down on social media.

Don't even ask them politely why they were so nasty. There is no upside to enacting any contact at all. You just have to rise above it.

In any case, the odd one-star review will demonstrate that most (if not all) of your reviews are legitimate.

- If you see a book on Amazon with less than ten reviews, all of five stars, you can be almost certain they are all friends and family.

- The first few reviews your book gets can be very valuable if they are constructively critical. So, keep an eye out for a pattern of worthwhile feedback.

- Similarly, look at the reviews your competitors get. See what people liked and what they didn't like about their books.

- You can study these reviews while writing your book, and address some issues or shortfalls in your own work before publishing.

- Reviews will help your Sales Rank and your book's visibility on Amazon as the algorithm will identify keywords that feature in reviews.

- **Top Tip:** Giving your eBook away for free in exchange for a review is perfectly fine, but you must never pay anyone to write a review for your book. Paying for reviews is a violation of Amazon's Terms of Service.

Chapter Twenty-One
Amazon Advertising

THE NEXT ELEMENT in your promotional strategy is advertising your book on Amazon.

The key to selling books on Amazon is visibility. You must get your book cover in front of as many members of your audience as possible, and the best way to do this is by advertising it on Amazon.

- Securing any significant visible presence is very difficult without advertising, particularly when you first launch.

- Advertising your book on Amazon is something you should always do and scale up as and when it is cost-effective and viable to do so.

- It is possible to advertise your book in most Amazon marketplaces, and these ads operate on a pay-per-click basis.

- The idea is that your book becomes more visible to people searching for a book like yours, possibly at the top of the search results and/or in the listings that run across the screen titled - Recommended for You or Related to this Title.

- If you look closely at any page of search results on Amazon, you will see the word Sponsored below some listings. These Sponsored Posts are all ads, and the publisher is paying each time someone clicks on their book cover.

- Amazon ads are another reason your Book Description needs to be first-rate, as you will pay each time someone clicks on your ad. And you may be paying a premium (if you choose) to see your ads at the top of the search results.

- Sponsored Posts operate on a bidding system and you will enter a bid that you are willing to pay per click for a Broad, Phrase, or Exact match to the keywords you have listed when you set up your ads.

- One of the benefits of advertising on Amazon is that it is the only time you will ever know how many people have clicked on your cover and visited your book's Detail Page.

- Short of charging you per click for your ads, Amazon will never share this information with you. As far as Amazon is concerned, people who visit your book's Detail Page are their customers, not yours, and they keep this data to themselves.

- You can, however, see how many clicks you have generated from your ads and compare this to how many sales your book has made.

- As a rule of thumb, you want to convert at least 1 in 5 clicks to a sale.

- 1 in 10 is borderline acceptable, as this will probably represent a financial break even on your ad spend.

- Anything worse than 1 in 10 and your Book Description isn't working, your reviews are poor, or the price of your book is too high. It may be a combination of all three, but it's most likely to be your Book Description.

- Importantly, when analyzing the performance of your Amazon Ads, make sure that you measure the results against all the book sales reported on your KDP Author Dashboard, not just those listed on your Amazon Ads Dashboard.

- The sales reporting on the Amazon Ads Dashboard is notoriously inaccurate, and given that sales resulting from ads improve your book's overall organic rankings, you need to consider the complete picture when analyzing the effectiveness of your ads.

I used to struggle when it came to analyzing the performance of my Amazon Ads, so I now use a tremendous resource that Amazon itself endorses and partners with.

It's called Publishing Performance.

Publishing Performance is an artificial intelligence program developed specifically to manage and enhance Amazon ads for books. The program will access your individual Amazon Advertising accounts in each marketplace and manage the entire process of creating, modifying, and optimizing your ads.

- Publishing Performance.

- Whether you decide to manage your own advertising or work with Publishing Performance, you will need to open an Amazon Advertising account in each Amazon marketplace where you want to advertise your book.

- To do this, select Promote and Advertise from the button on the right-hand side of the eBook listing on your KDP Author Dashboard, or click on the three dots to the right of the button that reads Order Author Copies for your paperback. Then select each Amazon marketplace (where you want to advertise), enter your personal and credit card details, and create an account.

- Sponsored Posts are your best option and reasonably easy to create. The hard part is when you come to analyze the data and determine which keywords are working for you and which bids need adjustment.

- If you are an experienced data analyst, familiar and comfortable working with complex spreadsheets, that's fine, but for many of us, this process is a confusing, complex, and frankly painful exercise.

- That's why I give the job to a sophisticated artificial intelligence program, which I can honestly say (Publisher Rocket aside) is just about the best investment I have ever made.

- Publishing Performance doesn't just manage the advertising process. It analyzes every element of your ad campaigns, finding ways to make them more cost-effective and generate more book sales.

- However, it is a learning process for the program, and it does take time, so be patient.

- Your ad spend will probably exceed your sales revenue in the first month or two. That should improve in your third, and by the fourth month, if you do not see a profit from your ads, then you almost certainly need to amend your Book Description.

- The Publishing Performance Dashboard is concise, simple, and user-friendly, while you can change your bidding strategy, keywords, and monthly ad budgets (in each Amazon marketplace) anytime.

A terrific resource I can recommend is an Amazon Ads course developed and presented by Dave Chesson of Kindlepreneur. I suggest you complete Dave's Amazon Ads course (which is free), as it will give you a solid understanding of the Amazon Ads platform.

You can then use that knowledge to manage your ads yourself or set them up with Publishing Performance.

- Kindlepreneur Amazon Ads Course:

Advertising on Amazon is an essential element in any author's marketing strategy.

Sales generated from ads will improve your book's organic rankings and increase your book's overall visibility and discoverability.

Remember, if you're not advertising on Amazon, your competitors probably are.

Chapter Twenty-Two
Other Opportunities

Audiobooks

NO BOOK FORMAT is growing faster than audiobooks.

If you own a smartphone, you own an audiobook portal.

When it comes to distribution, you can make your audiobook exclusive to Amazon/Audible, or you can distribute your audiobook more broadly with Findaway Voices.

- Findaway Voices is an audiobook distributor, and just as Draft2Digital will distribute your eBook and Ingram Spark your paperback, Findaway Voices (which is owned by Spotify) will distribute your audiobook to any number of online retailers, including Audible, Apple, Google, and Storytel.

- Alternatively you can upload your audiobook exclusively to Audible. Doing so will mean that you secure a better royalty but you will be sacrificing a much broader distribution.

- When it comes to producing an audiobook, you have three options. Use a narrator, do it yourself or use an artificial intelligence program.

- It is possible to hire a narrator for a few thousand dollars. This cost will vary depending on the length of your book, and both Audible and Findaway Voices have sample recordings from experienced narrators on their websites.

- Rather than pay someone upfront, another option is to agree to a royalty split with a narrator. In this case, there is no initial fee. Instead, you agree to split your author royalties 50/50 with your narrator.

- For some time, audiobook distributors and retailers (including Audible) did not accept audiobooks created with AI narrations. That has changed recently with advances in AI technology and the fact that today, it is practically impossible to discern a human narration from one created with artificial intelligence.

- All the same, I believe that recording your own audiobook is a good option. It is easier than using artificial intelligence, more cost-effective than employing a narrator, and it is an excellent proofreading method.

- And you don't need to hire a recording studio. You just need to fashion some rudimentary soundproofing and invest in the right equipment.

- Find a quiet space at home and cover hard surfaces like walls and windows (particularly those in front and behind you) with rugs, blankets, and comforters. When I record, I drape these elements over laundry racks or bookshelves, and suspend them from hooks attached to door and window frames.

- Then, you can read the text of your book from a desktop computer and record it on a laptop.

- Alternatively, you can print a hard copy of your manuscript and record on a computer.

- To do this, you will need to download a program called Audacity (which is free) or use Garage Band, a program that is installed on most Apple computers.

- Audacity Audio Recording Software:

- It is very important to use a good-quality microphone with a USB connection, and a Pop Screen.

- Never use a computer microphone.

- The microphone I use is an Audio Technica ATR 2100x.

- Screw the arm of your Pop Screen onto a desk and adjust it so that it is an inch or so short of the microphone and placed a few inches from your mouth.

- A Pop Screen looks like it is there to protect the microphone. Instead, it cushions the sound of some letters and words, such as 'pop,' that might otherwise spike on your recording and distort the audio.

- Finally, fold a thick rug or blanket over your computer tower to cushion the sound of the fan.

- Try to record at the same time of day, keep a bottle of water to hand, and sit in a comfortable chair (with no wheels or castors) on a surface that is not likely to make any noise.

- Thereafter, Audacity or Garage Band will enable you to edit and cut audio tracks together and save them to a computer.

- Record your files according to the specifications outlined on the Findaway Voices and/or Audible ACX website and send those individual files to an audio engineer to 'master.'

When I first recorded an audiobook, I was amazed at how clean and crisp my original recordings sounded once an engineer had 'mastered' them.

ElevenLabs

A leading AI narration studio is called ElevenLabs.

- ElevenLabs AI:

ElevenLabs gives you the opportunity to upload a copy of your book as a PDF, ePub or a Word document and thereafter select a 'voice' from its library of narrators.

- Narrators featured in the library have uploaded professional recordings of their own voices (each lasting two to three hours), allowing the ElevenLabs software to 'clone' their voices, so that these same people can effectively narrate your book.

- There is a degree of direction and management involved, particularly when it comes to reproducing accents and expressing emotions in dialogue, still the support that ElevenLabs provides is second to none.

- You will need to subscribe to an ElevenLabs Creator Package, and learn how to drive things, still, if you are prepared to put in a bit of work yourself, you can produce a first-rate audiobook that you can upload to Audible or publish with Findaway Voices, for a fraction of the cost involved in using a professional narrator.

Audiobooks are becoming increasingly popular with the prevalence of smartphones, and this is something you should certainly consider once you have sold enough books to recover your initial investment.

In my experience, people don't search for audiobook titles as they would an eBook or paperback title. They seem more likely to search for the audiobook version of a book they already know of, or a book someone has told them about.

This is why I suggest you recover your initial investment from paperback and eBook sales before producing an audiobook.

Author Website

- In time, you may want to create an author website, but I suggest you start with a Facebook Page for your book or for yourself as an author, and then promote your book on other social media sites like Goodreads, Instagram, YouTube, TikTok, and X.

- Tell everyone you can about it, and above all, let everyone know when your eBook is free to download.

- Rest assured, you don't need a massive social media following to promote your book.

- What you do need is to enlist the support of people who do; namely bloggers and podcasters.

- Read blogs, listen to podcasts, and email the presenters, telling them how much you enjoyed their content. Reference some recent element to demonstrate that you read or listened to it, and offer to send them a free copy of your book.

- Always include a link to your book on Amazon in your email so they can see that you are a legitimate author.

- Don't ask them to do anything for you; just tell them you enjoyed their blog/podcast and offer to send them a free copy of your book.

- Hopefully, something will follow as a result. Bloggers may write a review and podcasters may offer to interview you.

- Facebook Ads are very expensive and unlikely to prove cost-effective. They are something to consider if you have written several books that constitute a series, and are already doing well with Amazon ads.

- Remember, people who see your ads on Amazon are looking to buy a book. People who see your ads on Facebook probably aren't.

Translations

- Before you have your book translated study the Amazon search data in individual countries and see how many English language titles you have already sold in those countries.

- You may want to start with Germany. It is the most significant non-English speaking book market on Amazon, and you can access German search data from Publisher Rocket. All the same, your book may have a specific relevance or appeal to people in other countries.

- I wouldn't rush into getting your book translated. You should only consider a translation once your English language title is a success, and you may be able to grant the translation rights to a traditional publisher, while you continue to publish the English version of your book yourself.

- Above all, if you do employ a translator, don't shop around and try to save money. Use an established, professional translation service and find someone fluent in that language to proofread your manuscript. It's very easy for so-called 'translators' to upload your manuscript to Google Translate and simply copy the text. If that happens, native speakers who buy your book will be left feeling very disappointed and very unhappy.

Book Trailer

A fun and worthwhile marketing concept is to create a Book Trailer, which is a video that might comprise a series of royalty-free images that you downloaded from sites like:

- Shutterstock:

or

- Deposit Photos:

A Book Trailer is also an excellent way to show off the animated book cover that Damonza created for you.

You can download music for free from the YouTube library, and record a voice-over yourself or find a narrator on Fiverr.

Below is a link to a trailer I created for my book Positively Pazzo:

- Positively Pazzo Book Trailer:

And this is a link to an article about creating Book Trailers from Kindlepreneur:

- How to Make a Book Trailer:

My video editor is a fellow named Jason, and he does a tremendous job.

You can find him on Fiverr via this link.

- Fiverr - Video Editor - Jason:

Chapter Twenty-Three
Summary

WRITING A BOOK is one of the most worthwhile and vital things anyone can ever do, and those who undertake the task deserve every success that follows.

Not every book can be a bestseller, but I believe the information in this book can help you to achieve just that.

Social media, blogs, and podcasts all have their place when it comes to creating an awareness of your book and generating traffic to your book's Detail Page on Amazon.

Still, nothing will ever replace the solid fundamentals of book marketing:

- Audience

- Book

- Cover

- Description

- Keywords and Categories

- Amazon Ads

And nothing will ever compensate for a lack of them.

I wish you every success with your writing and publishing journey, and if this book has helped you in any way, then perhaps you would be kind enough to leave a short review on the website where you bought it.

Just a few words would be tremendous.

Reviews help more than you will ever know.

All the best and good luck.

Michael Francis

www.ingramcontent.com/pod-product-compliance
Lightning Source LLC
Chambersburg PA
CBHW071235070526
44583CB00017B/2189